A WORLD OF LUCK

Cover: Nature's emblem of luck, the four-leaf clover, rests among the gaming dice of human chance.

A WORLD OF LUCK

By the Editors of Time-Life Books

TIME-LIFE BOOKS, ALEXANDRIA, VIRGINIA

CONTENTS

GAMES AND GAMBLING

ames of chance are as age-old as the gods themselves, according to the ancient Greeks. On Mount Olympus, that realm of deities, a dalliance between the chief god, Zeus, and Tyche, goddess of fortune, produced a daughter, whom they named Gaming. From her tenderest years, she delighted in inventing games of chance and watching the chaos and discord they spawned.

Nevertheless, Gaming was fascinating and had many admirers. Her mother lit the daughter's palace with bright lamps that burned all night, and Gaming was never without giddy company. According to some accounts, she gave birth to twin sons, Dueling and Suicide, who followed her guests to the door of the pleasure palace as they left—grim company indeed for those who followed Gaming's wanton ways.

1

Dicey Business

The soldiers who knelt beneath Jesus' cross and cast lots for his clothes surely represent the low point of the use of dice. But if their deed was uniquely abhorrent, their method was commonplace. Dice, by all accounts, were among the first objects created specifically to summon, interpret, or manipulate fate. In ancient times, dice helped pass the time, make decisions, distribute property, and even commune with the gods.

The ancient Egyptians and Greeks both made dice called astragals from animal bones. Astragals are still used in the Arab world today, but dice have taken other forms as well, from golf-ball-size, many-sided pieces once used in Egypt to tiny cubes, a fifth of an inch across, used in China. Today's familiar six-sided dice, with the opposite sides adding up to the lucky number seven, have been in use since at least 1573 BC.

In Egyptian legend, Nut, the goddess of the sky, used dice to escape a curse laid upon her by Ra, the sun god. Ra, angered that Nut had wed her twin brother, Geb, declared that she would not be able to bear a

Incised on the lid of a 2,340-year-old bronze mirror case, Greek deities Aphrodite and Pan gamble using animal knucklebones, an early form of dice. A fourteen-sided die *(below)* was used by the Romans, who also employed more modern-looking cubes *(upper and lower left)*.

child on any day of the year. Thoth, the god of magic, pitied Nut and played dice with the moon on her behalf. The stakes were a portion of the moon's light. Thoth prevailed, and he added his radiant winnings—the equivalent of five days' light—to the Egyptian year, then 360 days in length. Thus Nut was able to have five children, and the world gained a 365-day year.

Dice figured in Greek myth, too. It was said that the gods rolled dice to divide up the universe, with Zeus winning earth, Poseidon the seas, and Hades the underworld.

Today's dice games are somewhat more mundane. In the United States, the favorite is craps, a two-dice game derived from the English game of hazard and developed by black Mississippi riverboat gamblers in the nineteenth century. In craps, the shooter wins if he rolls a seven or an eleven, both "naturals" in gaming parlance. He loses if he rolls a two, three, or twelve. If on his first throw he tosses a four,

five, six, eight, nine, or ten—his "point"—he shoots again until the game is resolved. He wins if he rolls his point again before he throws a seven, and he loses if he rolls a seven before repeating his point.

Craps is fast, entertaining, immensely popular, and, in many places, illegal. Craps has been blamed for many ills and social disasters, including the great Chicago Fire of 1871. Tradition holds that Mrs. O'Leary's cow was responsible for the conflagration, having kicked over a lantern in the barn. But another possible explanation surfaced several decades later: A Chicago businessman named Louis Cohn claimed in his will that he had knocked over the lantern himself during a particularly exciting crap game, then laid the blame on the heifer. Cohn regretted his act. "When I knocked over the lantern," he wrote, "I was winning." □

**Chinese women play at the game
wei-qi in an eighteenth-century painting from the Ch'ing period.**

The Power Game

Emperor Yao, ruler of China around 2300 BC, had a problem: His son was a bit feeble-minded, and the emperor feared that the young man would lack the skills necessary to run a kingdom. Yao's canny solution, according to the Confucian classics, was to invent *wei-qi*, a game of war with hundreds of playing pieces representing weapons and armies. With this elaborate diversion, the lad could amuse himself and at the same time learn the art of military strategy.

Wei-qi had a wider future in the governance of ancient China: It was used to decide such important policy issues as the selection of provincial rulers. It also spread far beyond the bounds of officialdom as a source of entertainment. The Japanese delighted in the game, calling it go. Some scholars speculate that wei-qi was an antecedent of chess; a war game similar to wei-qi lives on today in the German game kriegspiel. □

Descent into Disaster

Of the many tales of calamitous gaming losses, none has a more nightmarish finality than a story told in the *Mahabharata*, an Indian epic written around 300 BC. Its central figure is Yudhishthira, a warrior-prince of a mighty family, the Pandavas. A rival family, the Kauravas, conspires to steal his kingdom and stages a great feast for that purpose. There, Sakuni, the cleverest gambler among the Kauravas, challenges Yudhishthira to a game of *coupun*, in which dice are thrown from a box.

Yudhishthira, mindful of Sakuni's reputation, balks at the idea. But Sakuni says, "If you are so fearful of losing, you had better not play at all." Ever the proud warrior, Yudhishthira angrily replies, "I have no fear either in play or in war."

Alas for Yudhishthira, the dice are loaded. First, he loses a beautiful pearl, then a thousand bags of gold, then a piece of gold so pure that it is as soft as wax, then a chariot set with jewels, then slaves, cattle, his land, and the whole of his kingdom.

His ministers urge him to stop, but Yudhishthira will not listen. He gambles away his brothers' wealth, then his brothers' freedom, consigning them to slavery. He wagers his own freedom and loses. Sakuni says, "You have done a bad act, ◊

Yudhishthira, in gaming away yourself and becoming a slave. But now, stake your wife, Draupadi, and if you win the game you will again be free." Despite the cries of his relatives, Yudhishthira accepts this challenge—and loses again.

Utterly ruined, the stricken prince and his family are forced to go into exile. At this turn of events, Draupadi draws her long black hair in front of her face and vows to leave it so until the Kauravas are slain.

Years later, the Pandavas return to wage war on the Kauravas in an effort to regain their kingdom. So bitter is the fighting that it costs the lives of almost all members of both clans. The chain of disasters ends at last—in a bloodbath. □

A 1761 drawing shows the ruined Pandavas heading into exile.

Roman wrestlers grope for mastery in this ancient bronze sculpture.

Man to Man

Human fighting is very likely the world's oldest spectator sport. Both Egyptian and Chinese art of the second millennium BC depict wrestlers in action, and contests of strength between men were doubtless staged long before that.

In the first century BC, a Korean wrestler named Kehaya boasted that he was the strongest man alive. Another wrestler, Shikune, took the challenge and beat Kehaya, then proceeded to break the bones in his body one by one until Kehaya died. The emperor rewarded Shikune with a high office.

In AD 858, the kingdom of Japan was bet on a wrestling match. The emperor Buntoku had two sons, Koreshito and Koretaka. To establish the line of succession, a match was held between two professional wrestlers who served as proxies for the princes. Koretaka's wrestler lost, and Koreshito inherited the throne.

Boxing was formalized by the ancient Greeks. They wrestled as well but contended that boxing was a sport inspired by the gods. To limit injuries, light gloves were used, and the opponents wore belts to indicate the territory of foul blows. The Romans made boxing a more brutal affair, adding a heavy spiked glove called the cestus. At the end of a round, the ring would be covered in blood.

Boxing faded from fashion until the seventeenth century, then revived as bareknuckle pugilism. It retained a somewhat unsavory reputation until 1867, when the eighth marquis of Queensberry proposed rules that harked back to ancient Greece. He called for padded gloves, two- to three-minute rounds, rest periods, and a ban on blows below the belt—rules that form the basis of boxing today. □

High-Rolling Romans

From the loftiest patrician to the lowliest plebeian, the society of ancient Rome had a passion for gambling—most feverish at the very top. The emperor Augustus was accused by contemporary satirists of trying to compensate for his defeats on the battlefield by winning at dice.

Augustus was succeeded by his stepson Tiberius, who preferred pornography to gaming as a pastime. Gambling fever returned to the throne, however, with the advent of Caligula, maddest and baddest emperor of them all. When not busy killing his kin or installing his favorite horse in high public office, Caligula liked to wager, and for stakes he went beyond the treasury: He simply seized the property of wealthy citizens to support his habit. His equally addicted if somewhat saner successor, Claudius, had the interior of his carriage redesigned so that he could play dice while traveling. (The contemporary dramatist Seneca concocted a suitable hell for this emperor; he wrote a play in which

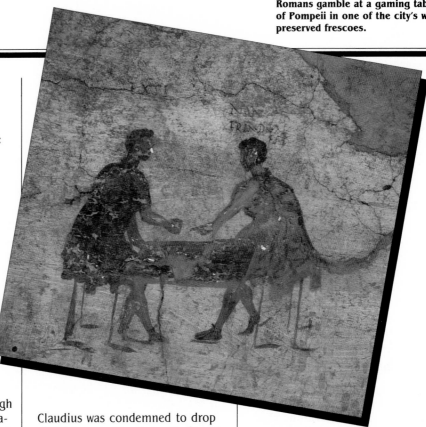

Claudius was condemned to drop dice into a bottomless cup for all eternity.) Nero, the next emperor, was the highest of rollers. Tapping the public treasury, he regularly wagered the equivalent of $50,000 on a single throw of the dice.

Roman courtiers quickly realized that skill at the tables delivered access to power. Commoners tried to emulate the pastimes of the mighty, too; archaeologists have found impromptu gambling tables scratched on just about every flat public surface in ancient Rome, including the Forum, the corridors of the Colosseum, and the steps of the temple of Venus. So rampant was the vice of gaming that some historians consider it to be one of the flaws that led to the empire's downfall. □

Military Distractions

The Goths and Huns were formidable foes of the Romans, but these tribes might have damaged the empire even more had not a taste for gambling blunted their appetite for conquest. One incident sums up their inability to resist a bet. In AD 250, a band of Goths defeated a Roman patrol but then agreed to risk a reversal of the battle on a coin toss. The Goths lost and were taken prisoner by the very troops they had just beaten.

A Roman soldier who had fought the Huns reported: "They are quick to anger, but easily appeased with a game of dice or a stake upon a race of chariots. Not one of them was ever known to cut off his thumbs to avoid the service of Mars"—a grisly Roman way of evading military conscription—"but they have tumbled themselves into our very prison camps for the sake of the wily Fortuna." The seductive Fortuna was the Roman goddess of luck. □

Long Suits

The origins of playing cards are murky, but theories suggest lusty beginnings.

Some historians believe cards were invented about 1,000 years ago to amuse concubines in China. These cards were slender paper rectangles that resembled dominoes in design. They were decorated with dots in black and white. Other experts contend that the fretful wife of an Indian maharajah devised cards as a distraction to break her husband of the annoying habit of tugging his beard. These cards were round and bore depictions of Hindu allegories.

By the thirteenth century, playing cards had made their way to the Middle East. The oldest surviving cards are hand-painted Islamic ones from fifteenth-century Egypt and are now housed in the Topkapi Museum in Istanbul, Turkey. The deck is fragmented, but clearly it once consisted of fifty-two cards arranged in four suits—coins, cups, swords, and sticks.

In less than a century, these suits had traveled to Europe, where they underwent various metamorphoses. The Germans, for

Domino-like dots ornament the nineteenth-century Chinese cards at left. The jack at right is from a sixteenth-century French deck.

instance, came up with suits of leaves, acorns, bells, and hearts, and are still using the symbols today. It was the French, however, who devised what came to be the definitive emblems, intended originally to reflect the four classes of society: Hearts for the church (the heart of the social order), spearpoints for the army (their resemblance to spades presumably accounts for the English name), diamond-shaped tiles for merchants (such tiles paved their crypts), and cloverleafs for the peasants (the English term *clubs* is of uncertain derivation).

For 500 years, these suits have withstood all challenges to their status as the norm, fending off would-be replacements that were usually inspired by politics. In revolutionary France, for example, symbols were created to denote liberty, equality, fraternity, and health. In Russia after the Bolshevik Revolution, presidents, commissars, industrialists, and workers temporarily ousted the old suits. Such upstarts did not, however, develop appreciable followings. □

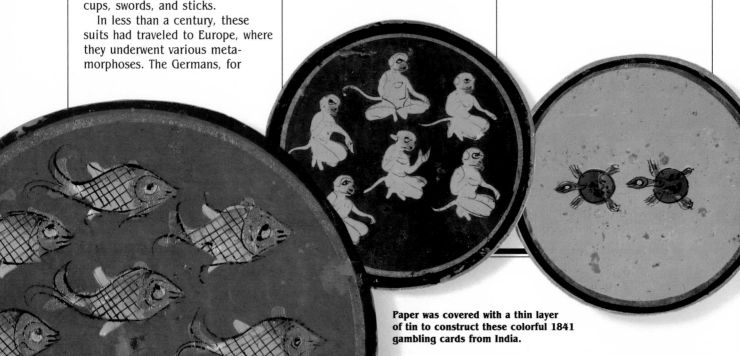

Paper was covered with a thin layer of tin to construct these colorful 1841 gambling cards from India.

Poker's Persian Patriarch

A Persian game called *as-nas*, which is at least 400 years old, may well have prefigured some of the most popular modern card games, although evolutionary shuffling has obscured the connections. The as-nas deck had five suits with at least four identical cards in each. The player's aim was to get specific card combinations, suggesting an ancestral relationship between as-nas and gin rummy, the three-card German game of *Pochen* and its French cousin *poque*, and modern poker games.

Poker's long bloodlines are thoroughly mixed with many stocks, however. Games other than as-nas contributed a number of poker's features, including the ante, the draw, straights and flushes, wild cards, and the use of the joker. □

Persian *as-nas* cards from the seventeenth to the nineteenth century were made of lacquered papier-mâché.

13

Unlucky gambler Henry VIII of
England gazes somberly from
a seventeenth-century portrait.

Food for Folly

John Montagu, the fourth earl of Sandwich (below), was British First Lord of the Admiralty during the American Revolution. However, the earl has gone down in history not for his martial skills but for an incident at one of his marathon gambling sessions. In 1762, at the age of forty-four, Sandwich sat down at the gaming table for twenty-four hours straight, refusing to leave even for meals. Instead, he commanded that meats and cheeses be put between slices of bread so that he could eat with one hand and play with the other. The result, of course, was the sandwich. This culinary expedient was not a first—the Romans had eaten such snacks—but it took a gambling aristocrat to give it a name for the ages. □

Henry's Habit

King Henry VIII of England was a man of prodigious appetites, and gambling—chiefly with dice—ranked high among his joys. Shrewd courtiers took shameless advantage of this craving: They imported professional gamblers from France and Lombardy and no doubt shared in the profits that the pros plucked from the king.

Henry had no shame when his wager lust was aroused. Once, he bet the bells of Saint Paul's Cathedral against £100 on one roll of the dice—and lost. Sir Miles Partridge, the winner, collected on the bet, even though it meant having the bells broken to get them out of the cathedral's tower. Bell metal was a prized commodity in those days, and Partridge probably sold the pieces for scrap.

The profligate Henry finally concluded that gambling was a social ill—in others at least. In 1541, he instructed Parliament to pass the Unlawful Games Act, which curbed "dicing, table, or carding" among ordinary folk. Gentlemen, of course, were exempt. Still, Henry's gambling prohibitions were not rescinded until 1960. □

Lady Luck's Lover

The eighteenth-century Venetian adventurer Casanova ranks as one of history's most energetic lovers, but he may have loved lucre more than ladies: He needed money for his true passion, gambling.

In 1745, at the age of twenty, Giovanni Giacomo Casanova made a career decision. "I had to earn my living one way or another," he later wrote, "and I decided on the profession of gamester." Within a week he was broke, but he borrowed a new stake from friends and took his game on the road, traveling among the great cities of Europe. "Pleasure, gaming, and idleness were my usual companions," he would recall.

His favorite game was faro, in which players bet on the card the dealer will turn up next. Casanova had great stamina, standing at the table night and day, and was clever enough to win more often than not. When the cards turned against him, he had no qualms about accepting jewels from his mistress of the moment so that he might rebuild his fortunes.

Bold in all ways, Casanova had great breadth of vision. Over the arguments of many detractors, he persuaded King Louis XV of France to let him start a government lottery to raise 20 million francs for a new military school. On the first day of sales, he took in 40,000 francs at his ticket office alone. Receipts throughout France totaled 2 million francs that day, with a profit of 600,000 for the Crown. The school, l'École Militaire, was built and still exists today. □

Dead Man's Hand

Playing cards came to the New World with the Spanish conquistadors and soon spread among the native population—with unfortunate results. In 1795, a missionary complained that the Apache souls he sought had been thoroughly corrupted by card playing. "This is the first milk they sucked from the Christians," he wrote in dismay.

If gambling was a bitter gift, it had a gruesome payback in the form of some cards that, many decades later, came into the hands of an American army captain named E. M. Kingsbury, a trader at the San Carlos Indian Reservation in Arizona. Indians often made their own cards, painting the faces on bark or hide. But the cards that the captain encountered were too thin to be either material. When Kingsbury made inquiries as to their nature, he was told that they were made of tanned human skin, stripped from white men during the Indian Wars. □

These animal-hide cards were collected in 1885 on the San Carlos Indian Reservation in Arizona.

The Father of Monte Carlo

Were it not for a French stock speculator named François Blanc, Monte Carlo, that most glamorous of gambling meccas, might have been no more than another hamlet on the Mediterranean coast.

In a high-flying career that began in 1834, Blanc, along with his twin brother, Louis, made half a million dollars speculating in stocks. But scandal broke when it was discovered that their acumen was based largely on information purloined from the telegraph. The brothers Blanc decamped to Germany, where they built a casino in Bad Homburg, advertised widely, and made another fortune.

In 1863, the tiny principality of Monaco was teetering on the edge of bankruptcy, and Prince Charles had the casino's proprietor call François Blanc for help. (Brother Louis had died in the 1840s.) Blanc knew just what to do. He hired the architect of the Paris Opera to design a casino near the ocean and built a hotel and lavish gardens. The prince named it Monte Carlo in honor of the surrounding mountains and his royal self.

Initially, there was no easy way to get to Monte Carlo, either overland or by boat. Blanc invested in roads and the harbor, and the resulting influx of visitors brought the casino profits of $160,000 in

Monaco's opulent Monte Carlo casino (above) was created by the French speculator François Blanc (inset).

the first year. Within five years, a rail line had been built between the principality and Nice, and Monte Carlo had become the pinnacle of fashion among spagoers.

Monte Carlo's success stirred envy in nearby Nice; the newspapers there declared that the new casino was prompting an avalanche of suicides—so many that bodies were being dumped at sea. Blanc put some of the editors on his payroll to quiet the press attacks. But apparently there was some truth to the charges. One day when

Blanc was strolling through the gardens, he saw a man about to shoot himself. "Sir, you are no gentleman!" he exclaimed angrily. "If you wish to shoot yourself, go home and do it; not here!"

Legend has it that if casino authorities found a suicide victim on the streets, they would stuff his pockets with money to counter any talk about losses at the gaming tables. (At least one quick thinker is said to have sprinkled tomato paste on his shirt and sagged to the pavement in feigned death, only to revive miraculously a little later, his pockets full.) But Blanc's casino was far too splendid and amusing to be hurt by sermons about the wages of gambling. When he died in 1877, Blanc left a fortune of 72 million francs. □

The Floating Casino

In the nineteenth century, the Mississippi River was the golden highway of America, with hundreds of steamboats traveling the sinuous miles between New Orleans and St. Louis. Nobody rode it with more verve than the gamblers who worked the paddle wheelers, and no member of this breed was more colorful than George Devol.

Born in Ohio in 1829, Devol ran away at age ten to work as a riverboat cabin boy. At this tender age, Devol later wrote in his autobiography, he also learned to play cards—and to cheat. Quick-witted and even quicker with his fists, the tall, sturdy Devol could handle any situation, but he had a broad streak of kindness. Sometimes, after plucking a victim clean, he would quietly return money. He refused to gamble with youths but

was always happy to entertain a rich planter willing to play three-card monte at $1,500 a turn.

Devol also taught his servant, Pinckney Pinchback, the tricks of the trade. "Pinch" won so much at cards that he eventually quit working for Devol, entered politics, and became lieutenant governor of Louisiana during Reconstruction.

The outbreak of the Civil War disrupted the river trade, so Devol and his fellow gamesters founded a military unit they called the Black-legs' Brigade (a blackleg is a gambler who cheats) and offered their services to the Confederacy. They quickly abandoned the cause after being exposed to shelling in a skirmish.

"I think the whole war is simply boring," Devol proclaimed.

After the war, the riverboats failed to recover their former glory. Most professional gamblers took off for the California gold fields, but Devol lingered on his beloved Mississippi until 1885. He tried working passenger trains, but it just was not the same.

Over more than forty years, Devol reportedly won two million dollars, but he lost most of the money, largely because of a card game he could never master. "It is said of me that I have won more money than any sporting man in this country," Devol wrote in 1886. "I will say that I hadn't sense enough to keep it; but if I had never seen a faro bank, I would be a wealthy man today." □

George Devol *(above)* **taught his servant, Pinckney Pinchback** *(right)*, **gambling savvy that founded the fortune of the ex-slave's son who later served as lieutenant governor of Louisiana.**

Santa Fe's Gambling Queen

When American trappers and traders began visiting the Spanish Southwest in sizable numbers during the 1840s, they inevitably found their way to the gambling halls, or *salas,* that provided some of the region's liveliest entertainment. Of all these establishments, none had a more lustrous reputation (or would prove more important to American interests) than that of the flamboyant Doña Gertrudis Barcelo.

Known as La Tules—an affectionate diminutive of Gertrudis—she had come to Santa Fe from the countryside a decade earlier after killing a man who had murdered her husband. In time, she became a monte dealer, and such was her aptitude with the cards that she soon built up enough capital to buy a sala of her own—a large adobe building at the corner of San Francisco Street and Burro Alley. Santa Fe's leading citizens flocked to the place for its variety of games and the attentions of lovely ladies of doubtful virtue.

Presiding over her realm of carved furniture, Turkish carpets, and crystal chandeliers, La Tules was a regal presence, draped in satin and gold. Her dramatic flair found expression in gestures as well as settings. At an opulent ball, for example, she was accompanied by a female servant who, at her mistress's bidding, would fall to the floor as a living footstool. La Tules rode between Santa Fe and Taos, collecting the winnings from her string of gambling stands in a plush carriage protected by uniformed guards. At her feet was a chest filled with gold.

As the lover of Don Manuel Armijo, governor of New Mexico, La Tules would play a role when the United States decided to take the region by conquest in 1846. When the American army appeared, she urged Don Manuel to negotiate. Money, not political power, was her aim. He collected a handsome payoff and the Americans entered the city without firing a shot.

La Tules's sala continued to prosper, and she even loaned money to the newly arrived U.S. authorities when they ran a little short. At the same time, she stayed in contact with the territory's erstwhile Mexican rulers, covering her bets. When she learned that they were plotting an attack on Christmas Eve, she played her card, passing word of the plan to the Americans. Many of the conspirators were arrested, and Mexico never regained Santa Fe.

The Americans banned gambling in Santa Fe the next year but exempted one establishment: the sala of La Tules. She died in 1852 and was mourned at a magnificent funeral—choreographed by La Tules herself. Years later, treasure hunters still scouted the desert outside Santa Fe, searching for a shipment of La Tules's gold that was said to have been buried in the desert by couriers when they were attacked by bandits. □

Dangerous Games

In 1849, thousands of men rushed to California in search of fortune in the newly discovered gold fields. But one of the travelers who disembarked in San Francisco did not intend to grub his gold from the earth. Charles Cora vowed to strike it rich at the gambling tables.

The tall, mustachioed Italian-American was certainly well equipped to do so. He had already made a name for himself playing faro in New Orleans, Vicksburg, and Natchez, the great Mississippi River towns. Cora was a genius at the tables, having won upwards of $300,000; the other gamblers whispered that he had a sixth sense. He was accompanied on his westward migration by Arabella Ryan, a beautiful, hazel-eyed young woman he had met in a New Orleans bordello. She was the daughter of a Baltimore minister, who had thrown her out of the house when he learned she was pregnant. She was seventeen at the time. Her child died at birth, and Ryan turned to prostitution, but Cora arrested her downward slide. Soon she was known as Belle Cora, though not by benefit of clergy.

Frontier California was an arena worthy of the Coras' talents; gambling was the premier pastime, and hundreds of sporting houses catered to the miners' thirst for fast money and willing women. Charles Cora set to work fleecing the sheep of the mining camps, and Belle opened one of the finest bordellos in San Francisco. By 1855, the Coras had climbed to the top of the sporting trade and were moving among the city's political and professional elite—socializing that was to be their undoing. One night at the American Theater, William Richardson, a U.S. marshal, took offense at some bawdy conversation the Coras' presence had prompted. He asked them to leave. They refused. The incident sparked a quarrel between the two men, which ended in tragedy on November 18, 1855, when Charles Cora shot and killed Richardson.

Cora had picked a bad time to kill a federal law-enforcement officer. San Francisco was in the throes of a crime wave, and the city's newspapers fanned the fires of public indignation to the point that fifty armed deputies were required to guard Cora's jail to fend off a lynch mob. Belle Cora paid Colonel E. D. Baker, one of the nation's best trial lawyers, $15,000 in cash to defend her lover. He argued that Cora had fired in self-defense. The jury deliberated for forty-one hours, then gave up, hopelessly deadlocked.

The lack of a verdict further inflamed the populace. James King, a newspaper editor, called the outcome depravity. King, in turn, was lambasted by James Casey, a political rival, city supervisor, and publisher of his own broadsheet. The King-Casey feud escalated until Casey ambushed King outside his office one day, shooting him and wounding him seriously. Casey was taken to jail and placed in a cell next to Cora's. The gambler looked at Casey and said sadly, "You have put the noose around the necks of both of us." Cora's premonition was dead on the mark. A vigilante army of 2,600 men stormed the jail and seized Casey and Cora. On May 20, 1856, Cora went on trial before the vigilante committee. That afternoon, word reached the courtroom that King had died. Cora was summarily convicted; Casey's conviction followed that evening, and the two men went to the gallows two days later.

Belle Cora married Charles legally an hour before his death. She devoted the next six years to a vendetta against the vigilante committee. After her death of pneumonia in 1862, she was buried beside her husband. □

Gold-rush gambler Charles Cora *(inset)* and politician James Casey hang from the ropes of their vigilante executioners in 1856.

Madame Mustache

The professional gamblers of the Old West were a wandering species, and none more so than a mysterious Frenchwoman named Simone Jules. Madame Jules was first spied running a roulette wheel in gold-rush San Francisco in 1850. Women, particularly women in casinos, were a novelty there, and her beauty attracted flocks of men. "A woman's place is in the home and indeed not at the gambling tables," grumbled the *Alta California*, a local newspaper. "There is no clearer proof of this than the example of twenty-year-old Mme. Jules as roulette croupier in the Bella Union."

In 1854, Madame Jules vanished from view, but soon afterward, a dark-haired young woman appeared in Nevada City, California, a rough-and-ready mining town. She called herself Eleanore Dumont, but her slim figure and downy upper lip looked remarkably like those of the Frenchwoman Simone Jules.

Madame Dumont rented a room on Broad Street and opened a game of vingt-et-un, known to Yankees as twenty-one. She insisted that the miners wear jackets and temper their language—rules that, perhaps in deference to her stylish appearance, the clientele obeyed. Soon she opened a saloon, the Dumont Palace. When the gold gave out in Nevada City, Dumont moved on to other outposts in the California gold fields—Downieville,

Sierra City, Oroville, Yreka. A silver strike lured her to Virginia City, Nevada. Then new finds of gold drew her to Orofino, Lewiston, and Boise in Idaho, and Helena, Florence, and Butte in Montana. With the passing years, her looks faded and the hairs on her upper lip grew coarser. One callous miner dubbed her Madame Mustache. The sobriquet stuck.

As her beauty faded, so did the quality of her establishments. Madame Mustache diversified into prostitution and began to drink heavily. But she remained a woman of spirit. When a Missouri River steamer approached Fort Benton, Montana, carrying passengers stricken with smallpox, the madame strapped on her pistols, strode to the riverbank, and ordered the captain to shove off. She then led cheering onlookers back to a celebration at her saloon.

The lady is also said to have headed off a riot in Pioche, a mining town in Nevada. When unem-

Protecting her business, Madame Mustache fires on smallpox sufferers trying to enter Fort Benton, Montana.

ployed miners marched to attack Mexican workers who had been hired in their place, Madame Mustache kidded them until they realized the quarrel was with the mine owners, not the workers.

Madame Mustache's adventures ended in the gold-mining town of Bodie, California, in 1879, when some fellow professionals came into her gaming house and cleaned her out. That night, in a lonely cabin on the outskirts of the mining camp, she drank poison. She was forty-nine years old. The *Sacramento Union* reported: "Bodie: September 9. A woman named Eleanore Dumont was found dead today about one mile out of town, having committed suicide. She was well-known throughout the mining camps." □

Dostoyevsky in Darkness

The Russian novelist Fyodor Dostoyevsky might never have achieved such greatness had it not been for the crushing pressure of his gambling debts. From 1862 to 1871, Dostoyevsky played roulette with such abandon that he almost destroyed himself and his family. Yet during those same years, he created a series of masterpieces, including *Crime and Punishment, The Idiot,* and *The Possessed.* "I can see absolutely nothing sordid about a person's desire to win as quickly and as much as possible," he wrote in *The Gambler,* another product of this period—a tale of a compulsive gambler's descent into self-delusion and poverty.

It was as if he took those words as his credo. In 1867, Dostoyevsky and his new wife, Anna, spent a tortured summer at the German spa of Baden-Baden, where they lived above a noisome smithy. The author gambled constantly, suffered epileptic seizures, and quarreled with everyone in sight, including fellow novelist Ivan Turgenev, from whom he had borrowed money to cover a roulette loss. All of the income from Dostoyevsky's stupendous literary output went to the wheel, as did the couple's pawned clothes, watches, and jewelry.

"When there remained nothing more to put on the gaming table and when all our resources had been exhausted, Fyodor fell into a deep melancholy," Anna wrote. "He moaned, threw himself at my feet, implored

my forgiveness—for he was not unaware of the torment he had caused me—and seemed at the extreme limit of despair."

The couple managed to escape Baden-Baden, but Dostoyevsky gambled wildly for four more years. Then the horror came to an abrupt end. In April 1871, after awakening from a nightmare in which his father warned that he would suffer a terrible fate, Dostoyevsky wrote to

Anna that his gambling days were over: "A great work is being accomplished in me, a hideous fantasy that *tortured* me for ten years has vanished. I always had this dream of winning. I dreamed this seriously, passionately. Now it is all over! Now it has happened for the very last time!"

Fyodor Dostoyevsky never gambled again. □

A Fateful Hand

Wild Bill Hickok lived a life brimming with adventure: Legend has it that he was, at various times, a Union spy, a scout during the Indian Wars in the West, a peace officer in several frontier towns, and a performer in Bill Cody's Wild West Show. Yet Wild Bill earned his place in history not so much by how he lived as by how he died.

Late in the afternoon of August 2, 1876, Hickok was playing poker in the Number Ten saloon in Deadwood, a rambunctious mining town in the Black Hills of Dakota Territory. Wild Bill had not taken his usual seat against the wall—the place he preferred because it protected his back. One story has it that his friends made him sit with his back to the door as a joke. In any case, as he concentrated on his cards, a young drifter named Jack McCall came up behind him and shot him in the back of the head. In the pandemonium that followed, a friend picked up Hickok's just-dealt hand. He held two pairs—aces and eights. Ever since, aces and eights has been known as the dead man's hand.

It was widely believed that local gamblers had paid Jack McCall to kill Hickok, perhaps because they feared he would become the next marshal and crack down on illegal gaming. But their guilt was never established. Jack McCall claimed that Hickok had shot his brother. In Deadwood, that was excuse enough: McCall was acquitted by a citizen tribunal.

Like most runs of luck, however, McCall's ran out. He was retried by a federal court, convicted, and hanged in March of 1877. □

Uncharacteristically seated with his back to the door, Wild Bill Hickok falls to the pistol of Jack McCall in a contemporary illustration.

Gates's Gambits

John Warne Gates started his career in Texas in the 1870s as a thirty-dollar-a-month barbed-wire salesman. He wound up known to the world as Bet-a-Million Gates, the man who would bet on anything, anytime. He even bet on rain-drops, at $1,000 a drop; the winning drop was the one that ran down a window fastest.

After amassing a fortune with a barbed-wire company and a steel corporation, Gates showed himself the hard-hearted equal of any robber baron. He once sold 50,000 shares of his steel company, then sacked 15,000 men, claiming the steel business was terrible. The market slumped, and within weeks Gates bought back his shares for a song. Another time, Gates manipulated the shares in a railroad company so deftly that he made $15 million off financier J. P. Morgan.

Gambling was Gates's deepest joy, although—despite his nickname—he never bet $1 million at one go; the nickname was awarded by newspapers after Gates attempted to bet a million on a horse race at Saratoga. But Gates did play bridge at $100 a point or poker with a $50,000 limit.

Once, a Kansas City gambler showed up in Gates's office, saying that he represented a syndicate that wanted to play Gates at any sort of game; he had a $40,000 stake. Gates whipped out a gold piece and flipped it in the air. "Heads or tails," he said. "You call it." The Kansas City man lost.

Gates was not above rigging the odds, as shown by an impromptu contest when he was dining with wealthy Chicago playboy John Drake. Gates suggested that they dunk pieces of bread in their coffee and see whose piece attracted more flies, at $1,000 per fly. Gates won a small fortune; he had spiked his coffee with six lumps of sugar.

Through it all, he seemed only to get richer, although in one year's poker playing at the turn of the century, he lost nearly $1 million. Soon he found a business gamble that more than offset the losses. After oil was discovered in Texas in 1901, Gates began to buy wells. In 1902, Standard Oil offered to pay him $25 million for the properties. Gates just laughed. By the time of his death in 1911, Texas oil had helped raise his worth as high as $100 million. □

John W. "Bet-a-Million" Gates takes a moment from gambling to walk his dog.

Guns and Gambling

On the often-violent Western frontier, many a gambler's skill with cards was matched by a knack for gunplay. Never would this deadly duality be more clearly demonstrated than in the showdown at the O.K. Corral in the mining town of Tombstone, Arizona, on October 26, 1881. On one side of the encounter stood Wyatt Earp, a card dealer who also served as a U.S. marshal; his brothers, Virgil, marshal of Tombstone, and Morgan; and Doc Holliday, a gambler and sometime dentist who had become friends with Wyatt back in another wide-open town, Dodge City. Holliday was soft-spoken but not a man to cross: Everyone knew he carried two revolvers and a sawed-off shotgun, as well as a long knife slung down his back under his coat. The foursome were cronies of Tombstone mayor John Clunn.

Opposing the Earps were some cowboys and small-time rustlers who lived in the hills outside town and had the backing of county sheriff John Behan.

There were many reasons for bad blood between the two factions. The Earps and Clunn were Republicans; Behan was a Democrat. The Earps were Yankees; the cowboys were Southerners. And not the least of it, Wyatt Earp had taken up with Josephine Sarah Marcus, a woman who had come to Tombstone to live with Behan but had fallen for Earp instead. Things went from bad to worse when Holliday, who dealt cards at the Oriental Saloon, reached for his ever-ready pistols in an argument and made the mistake of shooting the owner, Mike Joyce, in the hand. Joyce quickly turned over management of the gambling operation to Sheriff John Behan.

Wyatt Earp, who had held a part interest in the saloon, was furious. He knew Behan had only $5,000 to back his enterprise. So Earp strode into the Oriental, sat down at the faro table, and promptly won $6,000, cleaning Behan out. Per-

Wyatt Earp *(left)* **and Bat Masterson** *(above)* **cleaned up at the tables and on the streets of the Old West.**

W.G.SHYVERS

ALSO SUNG IN THE GAIETY BURLESQUE "CINDER-ELLEN UP TOO LATE."

THIS SONG MAY BE SUNG IN PUBLIC, WITHOUT FEE OR LICENCE, EXCEPT AT MUSIC HALLS.

NEW EDITION WITH BANJO ACCOMPANIMENT.

MONTE CARLO MARCH ...... by KARL KAPS 4:
MONTE CARLO QUADRILLES - WARWICK WILLIAMS 4:
MONTE CARLO WALTZ ...... - WARWICK WILLIAMS 4:
MONTE CARLO POLKA ...... KARL KAPS 4:
MONTE CARLO PARODY Sung by W.P.DEMPSEY 6º. nett.

The MAN THAT BROKE THE BANK AT MONTE CARLO

Written & Composed BY Fred. Gilbert.

Sung by CHARLES COBORN.

Price 2/- net

Copyright.

FRANCIS, DAY & HUNTER.
LONDON, 142, CHARING CROSS ROAD. W.C.
NEW YORK,
T.B.HARMS 3, FRANCIS,DAY & HUNTER, INC 1431-3, BROADWAY

haps in retaliation, Behan arrested Holliday for the holdup-murder of a stage driver; Virgil Earp countered by charging two of Behan's cronies with the holdup.

The feud finally erupted when, after an exchange of threats, Wyatt, his brothers, and a newly deputized Holliday decided to take on four of the cowboys, Ike and Billy Clanton and Frank and Tom McLaury. When the two factions faced off across a strip of open land, neither Ike nor Tom was armed. Billy Clanton and Frank McLaury defiantly cocked their revolvers, and bullets and buckshot began to fly. Wyatt shot Frank McLaury, the best marksman among the cowboys; Morgan Earp blasted Billy Clanton; and Holliday downed Tom McLaury with his shotgun. Virgil and Morgan Earp and Doc Holliday were wounded, but not grievously. Ike Clanton got away unscathed. The fight had lasted less than a minute.

Attempts at revenge were inevitable. Two months later, Virgil was caught in an ambush on a Tombstone street and crippled for life. Next, Morgan Earp was killed in a pool hall by shots fired through the glass of a back door. Wyatt, Doc, and their allies then stalked and killed four of their foes.

After this last blaze of gunfire, Wyatt and Doc fled to Trinidad, Colorado, where they met up with their old friend Bat Masterson, who was running a gambling room and serving as city marshal. He helped Holliday beat Arizona's murder charges. But Doc's time was running out; he died of tuberculosis in 1887. Wyatt Earp lived as he always had, gambling in one boom town after another across the West and in Alaska. He died peacefully in San Francisco in 1920. □

Bank-Breaking Labor

Fat, bald, and thoroughly unprepossessing, Charles Wells was described by the *Times* of London as "not a very fascinating personage." Perhaps not to the *Times*—but in 1892, the paunchy Englishman was a celebrity, immortalized in a hit song as "The Man That Broke the Bank at Monte Carlo."

Before he earned that exotic title, Wells made his living in London as a con man, selling false patents. After several investors questioned the whereabouts of the alleged inventions they had funded, Wells decided that another climate would be good for his health. In 1891, he appeared in Monte Carlo. He was an unknown when he arrived, but within weeks, strangers were inviting him to dinner and reaching out on the street to

touch his coat for luck; Wells had broken the bank an amazing three times playing roulette. The third time, Wells bet on every possible combination of the number five; he backed red and odd numbers and won 90,000 francs, cleaning out the house. As was the custom, play was stopped, and the croupiers solemnly draped a black cloth over the table. He had parlayed the £400 he brought to Monte Carlo into £40,000.

When Wells returned to London, he threw himself a victory dinner at the Savoy Hotel. The room was painted red, the waiters wore red, and only red food was served: prawns, lobster tails, ham mousse, red cabbage, and strawberries. When Wells reappeared at Monte Carlo in November 1891, he was ◊

25

welcomed back. Camille Blanc—son of the casino's creator and now its manager—did not think the bank breaker could possibly win again. Incredibly, Wells did, turning 120 francs into 98,000 with just one run—on the number five. His total winnings on that occasion came to 250,000 francs.

When Wells came to Monte Carlo yet again in January 1892, Camille Blanc himself presided over the roulette table. This time, Wells's winning ways deserted him, and the more heavily he bet to recoup, the more he lost. Eventually, Wells admitted that neither success nor failure derived from a system—he simply bet according to his instincts. Both victory and defeat came at the hands of Lady Luck.

Back in London, complaints about Wells's earlier shenanigans with patents prompted Scotland Yard to investigate him. In December 1892, he was arrested aboard his 291-foot yacht, the *Palais Royal*, in the Le Havre harbor. The Man That Broke the Bank had fallen on such hard times that he was selling the coal off his yacht.

Wells's attorney, Edward Abinger, argued that someone who could make £8,000 a day at roulette did not need to swindle investors. He also promised to reveal to the court Wells's system for winning. But he reneged, saying instead, "If I did, you would desert your wives and families, learned counsel would sell their wigs and gowns, and even His Lordship would forsake the judicial bench for Monte Carlo—and English justice cannot afford to lose its greatest figure."

Despite Abinger's adroit plea, Wells was convicted of fraud; he spent eight years in prison and died broke in Paris in 1926. □

The Million-Dollar Dollys

Young, beautiful, and ambitious, the Dolly sisters were a dazzling presence in French casinos during the gilded days of the 1920s, and they maintained their luster the old-fashioned way—on someone else's money.

The twin sisters, whose real names were Janzieska and Roszieska Deutsch, were Hungarian vaudeville and cabaret dancers. The American impresario Florenz Ziegfeld added them to his Follies revue in 1911. Shortly after World War I, the Dolly sisters were performing in a London club when they caught the eye of Harry Gordon Selfridge, an American-born department-store executive who had come to London at the age of fifty-three and founded a hugely successful store there.

Selfridge fell in love with Jenny Dolly and invited the sisters to his villa outside the French gambling resort of Deauville. He liked gambling, but the Dolly sisters loved it, and they were soon fixtures at the tables, playing with carefree glee. And why not? It was Harry's money. When they won, they would buy eye-popping jewels. They acquired a fifty-one-carat diamond. Rosie explained their purchase by saying, "It isn't safe for two girls to go home with all that money." When they lost, the sisters would ask Selfridge for more money; they gambled away two million pounds in seven years. Despite the cost, Harry remained indulgent, sending them diamonds and pearls to "make up for your losses last night, darlings."

Selfridge, a widower, begged Jenny to marry him, but she refused. Instead, after losing £100,000 in 1930, she announced that she was going to quit gambling and open a shop selling art objects on the Champs Élysées in Paris. The ever-devoted Selfridge financed the enterprise, but Jenny botched it. Within two years, the shop went out of business, and Jenny had to sell her fabulous jewels to pay her debts. For once, Selfridge was no help; although his store was still a gold mine, he was heavily in debt and threatened with bankruptcy. Without his support, Jenny soon went bankrupt herself. Far worse, her beautiful face was ruined in an automobile accident. Devastated, she killed herself. Her twin, Rosie, came to a happier ending. After two failed marriages, she found happiness in a third matrimonial venture and could still be seen in the 1950s at the gaming tables of Deauville, playing sedately where she had once dazzled the world. □

As high-spirited Dolly sisters Rosie *(far left)* and Jenny strike a pose, their benefactor, Harry Gordon Selfridge *(top)*, peers from a turn-of-the-century photograph.

Steep Thrills

The original Nick the Greek is dead, but "Nick the Greek" lives on, in lexicon and legend. To be like Nick the Greek means to have the lowdown, the inside track, the Midas touch—to be a shrewd and canny winner. The real Nick the Greek did indeed win—and lose—hundreds of millions of dollars gambling, but he is remembered as much for his flair for life, as for playing big and often.

Nicholas Andrea Dandolos was born in 1893 in Crete and was privately schooled in Izmir, Turkey, where his major interest was philosophy. At age eighteen, Dandolos set off to tour the world before enrolling in Oxford. He never got to the English university, however, because a stopover in Chicago changed his life. It was there that he met a young Greek-American woman and fell in love.

He planned to marry her after his tour, but in 1912, when he was in Montreal, he learned that she had died suddenly.

Despondent, Dandolos began drinking heavily and gambling, especially on horses. Despite losing at love, he seemed unable to lose at the track. Before his binge was over, he had won a million dollars—and, from the Daily Racing Form, the nickname that would follow him for the rest of his life: Nick the Greek. Although Dandolos stopped drinking, he never stopped gambling.

Over the following years, Nick gambled on a grand scale in cities across America. By the mid-1920s, his reputation as a major player set the stage for two legendary marathon gambling contests with high-stakes New York gambler ◊

and racketeer Arnold Rothstein *(next page).* The first confrontation took the form of a twelve-day crap game that cost Dandolos more than a million dollars. Nick left New York to refill his coffers elsewhere on the gambling circuit, then returned to challenge Rothstein to a series of pitched poker battles. At one point, Nick was leading by a wide margin, but a single losing hand of stud poker cost him $605,000, and he wound up losing almost $800,000 in all. Afterward, Nick looked at Rothstein and said, "You gamble for greed. I gamble for thrills."

"But you can't eat thrills," Rothstein replied.

"True," said Dandolos, "but neither can you replace them by anything." In truth, Nick gave away a great deal of his money; ci-gars were his chief personal luxury.

Nick the Greek was a legendary figure in Las Vegas casinos. In 1949, he sat down to play poker with his archrival, Johnny Moss *(pages 35-36).* The game lasted for four months, with breaks every four or five days to sleep. It ended with Nick out two million dollars.

That setback was the start of a long losing streak. He spent his last years playing five-dollar-limit draw poker in California cardrooms. When a fellow player asked how the one-time king of gamblers could stoop so low, Nick replied, "It's action, isn't it?" He died on Christmas Day, 1966—broke, but without regrets. "The next best thing to gambling and winning," he once declared, "is gambling and losing." □

Greeks Bagging Gifts

In 1919, two Greeks and an Armenian pooled their resources to form a gambling powerhouse that would be called the Greek Syndicate. Joined by two more members—another Greek and a Frenchman—they dominated European casino gambling for decades, taking turns at the baccarat tables and reaping riches from the deepest pockets of the day.

Much of the syndicate's success could be ascribed to its leader, Nico Zographos. The son of a Greek professor of economics, Zographos had an exceptional memory, which served him well at baccarat. In that game, six decks—312 cards—are shuffled and dealt out of a box called a shoe. When fewer than nine cards remain, six more decks are added. Zographos could often name the last few cards left, having kept track of all the others as they left the shoe. He also maintained a huge mental store of players' previous bets and psychological quirks.

In 1922, the syndicate inaugurated no-limit baccarat at the Deauville casino in France. Zographos announced he would cover the biggest bet anyone cared to make. High rollers such as Gordon Selfridge *(pages 26-27)* and King Farouk of Egypt wagered eagerly, and the syndicate's income grew by leaps and bounds, with an estimated one billion pounds passing through Zographos's hands alone.

The syndicate had some bad runs, of course. In 1926, for example, its members lost $672,000 in a week's play at Cannes. Two years later, however, Zographos bet one million francs on a hand—and won. The victory card, a nine of diamonds, became his insignia.

World War II put the Greek Syndicate out of action, but after the war the group took in some new members and continued the lucrative harvest. Zographos died in 1953, leaving a fortune of more than five million pounds. When the last of the original members passed away in 1962—the Frenchman, François André—2,500 letters and telegrams arrived from all corners of Europe, paying homage to the masters of the baccarat tables for almost forty years. □

Little Al from Jersey

A man of wide acquaintance, Nick the Greek Dandolos once had occasion to escort the great physicist Albert Einstein around Las Vegas. Einstein was a member of the Institute for Advanced Study at Princeton at the time.

Nick wanted his visiting genius to be treated with respect, but he was mindful that certain members of his own gambling circle might not be thoroughly conversant with the world of science. Hence, he introduced Einstein as "Little Al from Princeton—controls a lot of the action around Jersey."

It is recorded that Einstein, though much amused, managed to keep a straight face. □

The King of the World

"The majority of the human race are dubs and dumbbells," said Arnold Rothstein *(below)*, a gamester, fixer, and all-around thug in New York during the 1910s and 1920s. But if he thought most people fools, Rothstein saw himself as a breed apart. His modest ambition, he often said, was to be king of the world. And indeed, his own mental abilities were exceptional. Highly intelligent, tireless, and ruthless, he made big money as a gambler in his teens and went on to build an empire that included saloons, real estate, and a variety of unsavory enterprises that ranged from loansharking to rumrunning and drug trafficking.

In gaming, he was similarly eclectic: He played poker, craps, roulette, pool, the horses—anything at all—and the higher the stakes, the better. One winning poker hand brought him $605,000; a win at the track in 1924 paid off to the tune of $800,000.

Rothstein's innumerable shady exploits may have included fixing the 1919 World Series between the Chicago White Sox and the Cincinnati Reds. It was alleged that he paid $100,000 to some White Sox players to throw the series. Said Rothstein, who won $350,000 betting on the Reds, "I have never been connected with a crooked deal in my life." This claim was greeted with general amazement, but his involvement was never proved.

Rothstein finally came to grief on November 4, 1928, when police found him collapsed in the service entrance of New York's Park Central Hotel, a slug from a .38-caliber pistol lodged in his abdomen. The authorities soon figured out that Rothstein owed $340,000 from a poker game but had refused to pay because he thought he had been cheated—or so he said. More probably, he did not pay off because he did not have the cash on hand. Faithful to the underworld code, his only comment to the police was, "I got nothing to say."

After lingering for two days, Rothstein died of his wound on November 6. It was an election day, and one with a certain ironic significance. Herbert Hoover won the presidency that day, and Rothstein—who bet on elections just as he bet on everything else—had put big money on Hoover. The gambler died on a day when he would have netted more than half a million dollars, more than enough to solve the cash flow problem that killed him. □

Playing the Ponies

Racing horses and betting on them arose with the dawn of civilization. As long as 6,000 years ago, desert tribes in the Middle East raced horses without riders. The ancient gamesters deprived the animals of water and set them free to run, thirst-maddened, to the nearest spring. One such race, offering a prize of 100 camels, proved a bit too exciting. As the two fastest horses began to pull away, the spectators threw rocks at the laggards to speed them up. The rock-throwing ploy degenerated into a melee, setting off a war between two tribes that lasted a century.

By 2300 BC, the Egyptians were staging lively contests complete with grandstands, jockeys, and sizable purses. The ancient Greeks and Romans acquired a taste for horse racing from peoples of the Near East. In Rome, as many as fifty races a day—both chariot contests and races with riders—were held in the Circus Maximus, an enormous arena that held 350,000 spectators.

The first public horse races in Europe were run in England in the twelfth century, at the horse fairs just outside London. Eventually, such diversions would come to be known as the sport of kings, and many of the wagers were regal indeed. Richard the Lion-Hearted once offered the handsome sum of forty pounds of "ready gold" on a single bet. Five hundred years later, another English monarch, King Charles II, was indirectly responsible for exporting horse racing to America. King Charles appointed as colonial governor of New York one Richard Nicolls, who,

in 1665, ordered a racetrack laid out at Hempstead, Long Island. He called it Newmarket, after an English track that Charles had helped to popularize.

In early America, informal racing was a proving ground for animals that were vital in the transportation of the day; the fastest horses commanded the highest stud fees. But racetracks dedicated to the age-old cause of entertainment quickly sprang up throughout the colonies, growing into large-scale operations by the nineteenth century. In 1870, tracks in New York alone drew $15 million in bets.

Spectators climb stools to watch the action at Brooklyn's Gravesend racetrack a decade after a bizarre conflict pitted bookies against the track.

By then, most wagers were handled by bookmakers, who paid a daily fee to the track to operate there, knew the horses and riders, and not infrequently could manipulate the races to their advantage. But plenty of action also took place in off-track "poolrooms," which received up-to-the-minute results by telegraph. This critical flow of information between track and poolroom was the cause of one of the more colorful episodes in racehorse history: the Great Battle of Gravesend.

In 1891, the Brooklyn Jockey Club, which ran the races at Gravesend track in Brooklyn, announced that it was quadrupling the $1,000-a-day fee that the poolrooms were being charged for telegraphed race results. Outraged, the bookies refused to pay; they sent runners to the track to collect the results. Philip Dwyer, president of the Brooklyn Jockey Club, countered by calling in 130 Pinkerton guards to prevent anyone from leaving the track before all the day's races were over. The bookies then tried spying into the track from nearby buildings. Unfortunately, the view of the finish line was blocked. To deal with this problem, they had operatives inside the track hold up numbered placards in the order in which horses had finished. The Pinkerton guards disrupted this information channel easily enough, and they also intercepted tactical missiles that the bookmakers' operatives lobbed over the walls—hollow balls containing the race results.

To minimize the possibility of leakage, Dwyer built a sixty-five-foot fence around the track. The bookmakers responded by erecting a tower on the roof of a nearby hotel. Dwyer promptly raised his fence.

Just when it began to look as though Dwyer had victory in his grasp, the poolrooms found a way around his defenses. The public could not figure out how the bookmakers had done it until a local newspaper ran the headline: "Electricity in the Hat. The Most Ingenious Scheme Yet for Obtaining Racing News." The accompanying article explained that a certain Joseph Frost, an electrician and president of the Automatic Fire Alarm Company, had been attending the races each afternoon in an elegant carriage. Frost had wired the top of his coachman's hat with a battery-powered light. The coachman tapped out Morse code on a hidden foot pedal connected to the light, and the visual signals were relayed to the poolrooms by telegraph operators watching from outside the track. The electrical hat continued its transmissions for six days before the Pinkertons learned of the ruse. With that, the war ended. Dwyer and the Pinkertons had won, although the feud continued at a low boil for a time in the form of lawsuits and countersuits. □

Poker and the President

Poker may have made Richard M. Nixon president. As a lieutenant commander in the navy during World War II, Nixon *(above)* spent most of his off-duty hours playing cards. One officer who served with him said the future president would engage in marathon games without ever displaying a flicker of emotion. "A hundred navy officers will tell you he never lost a cent at poker," he added. Nixon's winnings constituted a large share of the $10,000 stake with which he launched his political career.

In his memoirs, Nixon protested that his poker playing in the navy "has been somewhat exaggerated in terms of both my skill and my winnings. Any kind of gambling had been anathema to me as a Quaker. But the pressures of wartime, and the even more oppres-

sive monotony, made it an irresistible diversion. I found playing poker instructive as well as entertaining and profitable.

"I learned that the people who have the cards are usually the ones who talk the least and the softest," he asserted. "Those who are bluffing tend to talk loudly and give themselves away."

Although in retrospect Nixon downplayed his passion for poker, he apparently did not repent it entirely. The Nixon Library in Yorba Linda, California, displays a pair of deuces commemorating a notorious game in which Nixon won $1,500 on the strength of two twos and a steely-eyed bluff. □

Dream Bets

In March 1946, John Godley, a twenty-five-year-old student at Oxford University in England, dreamed that he saw some racing results in the next day's newspapers. On waking, he recalled two winners, Bindal and Juladin. He told several friends about this dream. Then, thinking that there might be something to it, he called a bookmaker, determined that a Bindal and Juladin were in fact in a race that day, bet forty pounds on them—and won.

Godley thought his premonition was a freak event. But a month later, he dreamed that a horse called Tubemoore would win the next day at Aintree, an Irish racecourse. No such horse had been entered, but a Tuberose was running. Godley and his friends bet on Tuberose at 100-6. They won.

That summer, Godley dreamed that he had asked his bookmaker for the results of a late race. The winner, said the bookmaker in the dream, was Monumental at 5-4. The next day, Godley found a horse listed as Mentores. He backed it. Mentores won at 6-4.

The next year, two more winners were suggested by a dream. He wrote them down, had the document witnessed, and deposited it in the safe of an Oxford postmaster. The horses came in as predicted—and Godley won a little extra by selling his story to the *London Daily Mirror*. He later worked briefly for the paper as a racing correspondent but quit when he found himself betting to excess.

Godley had two more winning dreams, plus one loser. Then his unconscious tipster went silent until 1958. During a visit to Monte

Carlo, Godley dreamed that the Grand National, Britain's greatest steeplechase race, was won by the third favorite, What Man. A little research revealed that a Mr. What was entered in the race, but when he found that the horse was not the third favorite, but a 66-1 long shot, Godley decided not to bet. On the day of the race, however, he picked up a newspaper and saw that Mr. What was now the third favorite at 18-1. He quickly bet £25. Mr. What won, and Godley was £450 richer.

That was the last of his horse-picking dreams, whose origin baffles him to this day. When he asked psychic researchers about his experience, they suggested—reasonably enough—that he may have subconsciously chosen winners during his waking hours, then dreamed about them at night. □

Rigged Record

Billy Fox was an honest and hard-working professional boxer, but his manager, Frank "Blinky" Palermo, subscribed to other values. Although Fox won fifty of his fifty-one bouts—even beating future middleweight champion Jake La-Motta in 1947—his record was less than met the eye.

Palermo, connected to the New York underworld, knew every trick. As Fox recalled, "The first funny thing happened when I fought this Larry Kellum, who I had already beat under his own name. This time he called himself Andy Holland." Usually Palermo did not bother with name changing: He simply added nonexistent bouts to his fighter's record. When Fox questioned him, Palermo said they were there for publicity.

The manager was also a master fixer, as shown by Fox's bout with LaMotta, who had never been knocked out in seventy-eight previous bouts. Strange fluctuations in the odds preceded the event. From the opening bell, LaMotta let Fox pound him mercilessly, and the fight was stopped in the fourth round—to jeers and hoots from the crowd. LaMotta would later admit to a Senate investigative committee that he had thrown the match with Fox in return for a promised shot at the championship in 1949. Fox was crushed. "I still feel hurt," he said much later.

"Why couldn't he have done it to a guy who didn't give a damn?" After that fight, Fox's career slid rapidly downhill, and in 1960, he was confined to a state mental hospital. □

Billy Fox lands a right uppercut on Jake LaMotta during a fixed 1947 fight won by Fox.

| | Player's advantage when the dealer's up card is | | | | | | | | | You have |
	2	3	4	5	6	7	8	9	10*	↓
						145	056	−040	−173	19
64	094	130	176	229	236	145	056	−04		18
93	095	130	177	230	239	144	057	−0		17
51	092	146	167	212	235	061	−021			16
	031	065	112	157	203	184	105			15
73	...	149	194	289	308	200	111			14
71	120	...	233	312	339	220	076			
74	126	195	...	358	378	186	081	−01.		
59	184	240	315	...	409	16.				
35	179	240	313	370	...					
54	171	236	289	233	232					
56	159	206	148	196	218					
33	131	067	124	181						
6	024	05.		137						
5	176	2		310						
4	249	2								
	186									

tural has b

Probability Play

In January 1961, a twenty-eight-year-old academician named Edward O. Thorp spoke to a meeting of the American Mathematical Society on an unusual topic. His talk was titled "Formula's Fortune: a Winning Strategy for Blackjack"—and it was just that.

Two years earlier, while on vacation in Las Vegas, Thorp had become interested in using the mathematical laws of probability to predict the odds on particular cards being dealt as a blackjack game proceeded. Then he took a job as an instructor at the Massachusetts Institute of Technology, where he struggled with the necessary computations, only to conclude that they would take "ten thousand man-years at desk calculators." Not so, said a colleague, who suggested that Thorp try the university's IBM-704 computer. He taught himself how to program the machine, then put it to work. Six months later, he had a book-length mass of data.

"The answers amazed me," Thorp later said. In blackjack, he discovered, the odds fluctuate between dealer and player as successive hands are dealt. He used the computer's output to devise an odds-gauging system based on counting face cards and tens (the cards most beneficial to the player) and also keeping track of fives (the cards most beneficial to the dealer). After he described his system to fellow mathematicians, the press got wind of it, and soon he was being offered large sums of money for a trial. He accepted a stake of $10,000, went to Las Vegas, and in thirty hours of play turned it into $21,000—an adventure he subsequently recounted in a book, *Beat the Dealer.* But the casinos had the last word. Seeing that they could not win against his mathematical logic, they instructed their dealers to shuffle cards and change decks more frequently, making it more difficult for Thorp to keep track of the cards. According to Thorp himself, one dealer went so far as to drug his drinks.

Eventually, when even these measures failed to defeat Thorp and his card-counting followers, most casinos simply declared themselves off-limits to the astute academicians. □

Mathematician Edward Thorp, sitting in front of his strategy tables, deals blackjack in a 1964 photo.

Showdown in Las Vegas

Every year since 1970, scores of the best card players on earth have gathered in a Las Vegas hotel to test their talents in the World Series of Poker. Of the many poker greats who have entered, none is more revered than Johnny Moss, a Texan who learned his card skills in the school of hard knocks.

Born in 1907, Moss became a professional gambler at the age of nineteen. "There wasn't much easy money in Texas in them days," he once said, "and gambling was a way out." High stakes were his style from the start: He won $100,000 playing poker in 1939 and told his wife to start shopping for a new house. Before she could find one, he told her to forget it; he had already lost the money. She eventually took over family money management.

In 1949, Moss came to Las Vegas at the invitation of his childhood friend Benny Binion, ◊

In his younger days, Andrew Jackson could not resist gambling on horse races and cockfights. He lost a sizable inheritance on these diversions, then averted financial ruin by winning big in a dice game called rattle and snap. Even as president, Jackson raced his horses near Washington, much to the chagrin of his advisers.

owner of the no-frills hotel where the World Series would be staged. Soon Moss was playing such legendary gamblers as Nick the Greek Dandolos, sitting at the tables for days and nights on end. Like all great players, Moss knew human nature as well as the poker odds. If he was up against a particularly stony-faced opponent, he would drop his cigarette and bend down to see if the other player's feet were tapping or knees were knocking—signs of a big hand or a bluff. In 1950, Moss won one million dollars playing poker in Reno, Nevada. After that, he had a hard time finding willing poker players, turned to dice games, and lost his entire stake. Friends loaned him $500,000 to get started again.

At the first World Series of Poker, in 1970, Moss was sixty-three, unusually old for a professional in a game that requires steel nerves and endurance. He won, won again in 1971 and 1974, and made it to the finals in 1980, at the age of seventy-three. When he stood up to leave that year, the other players at the table gave him an appreciative round of applause.

The main event in the World Series is hold 'em, a Texas variant of seven-card stud. Each player buys in for $10,000 and plays until he or she is tapped out. The game has no betting limit, and tens of thousands of dollars sometimes cross the table on a single raise. The 1990 World Series winner pocketed $835,000. One of the people the winner busted was Johnny Moss, still in the game at eighty-three. □

Johnny Moss, left, winner of the first World Series of Poker, in 1970, admires the tournament trophy with series host Benny Binion.

Rotisserie League baseball-team owners scout players at spring training in Saint Petersburg, Florida, in 1984.

Big Leagues, Small-Time

Professional sports are big business, with players' salaries reaching into the millions of dollars and teams selling for hundreds of millions. But a growing number of sports-crazy Americans are discovering that they can experience the joys and pains of team ownership for only a few hundred dollars. The secret: sports fantasy leagues. The first, a phantom football team, took root in California in the mid-1960s, the creation of Oakland Raiders fans. The first fantasy baseball team was started in 1980 by a group of enthusiasts whose favorite restaurant was La Rotisserie Française. The eating place yielded the nickname Rotisserie League, which applies only to phantom baseball teams.

The rules are simple. Would-be "owners" put up a modest sum of money to create a league—baseball, football, basketball, hockey, or whatever their particular enthusiasm. They then build their fantasy teams by a "draft" of players in the real leagues. Thereafter, statistics measuring the performance of these actual players determine standings in the phantom league. As the fantasy season progresses, players can be traded, waived, reactivated, and so on. Computers, newsletters, and the telephone ◊

are used to distribute information. At the end of their season, fantasy leagues hold banquets and award prize money.

Phantom sports leagues have been spawned by the thousands—but they are not without their perils. In 1989, police in Austin, Texas, raided Scholz's beer garden and arrested eight men for "engaging in organized crime." The men had invested $250 each in a fantasy football league and were vying for a payoff that could have been as much as $3,000 at season's end. The wife of one of the arrested men had called and complained that her husband had spent part of the rent money on his fee. Her distress notwithstanding, none of the men was held for more than a few hours, and none has been indicted on any charge connected with the raid.

Even in the remote event that anyone ever goes to jail for fantasy league gambling, that person may not necessarily be deprived. At least one Canadian prison—a maximum security facility in Ontario—has a fantasy football league operating within its walls. □

Horses are not the only animals used for gambling. In various parts of the world, gamesters race camels, goats, tortoises, crabs, frogs, and crawfish. Creatures pitted against each other in fighting contests include dogs, camels, fish, scorpions, snakes, and crickets.

THE ODDS ARE ...

What can happen will happen. Roll the dice; a seven will turn up. Spin the roulette wheel; it will stop on red. Buy a lottery ticket; the number will win a million-dollar jackpot. What can happen will happen: This is the gambler's credo, a certain faith that this ticket will win or those dice will not crap out. What can happen will happen: Above all, this is the mantra of mathematicians. They know the limits of certainty and calculate the slender odds on which the gambler's fortune rests.

Small World

Not long after the assassination of President John F. Kennedy in 1963, similarities were noticed between this and another calamitous event nearly a century earlier, the murder of Abraham Lincoln.

Lincoln was shot in Ford's Theater; Kennedy was killed in a Lincoln automobile, built by the Ford Motor Company. Both men were assassinated on Fridays; both had their wives at their sides. It was further noted that Kennedy's secretary was Evelyn Lincoln and that the names Lincoln and Kennedy both have seven letters. Both presidents were succeeded by vice presidents named Johnson, each with a six-letter first name; what is more, Andrew Johnson was born in 1808 and Lyndon Johnson in 1908.

And so it goes, a cascade of coincidence leading some to conclude that a common force was at work in both assassinations. Modern science, backed by mathematical theories and analyses, claims otherwise: Countless similarities exist between unrelated people and events—so many that their absence, not their presence, would be exceptional. Scientists, unlike seers, do not claim to know that a certain event will occur at a specific time or place—that John Jones will be dealt four aces in Friday's poker game, for instance. But some—those who study probability theory—can tell Jones how likely the hand is, allowing him to place his bets accordingly.

Although no event is really predictable, some do occur far more frequently than others, a few so often that even sophisticates are fooled. The Birthday Problem is a classic among statisticians. In this, two strangers meet at a party and discover that they share the same birthday; what a strange coincidence, they exclaim. The numbers tell a different story, especially if

the party is very large. In any group of twenty-three people, there is a fifty-fifty chance that two will have the same birthday. Invite fifty people to the affair, and the odds are thirty to one that two will share a birthday. Double the size of the party to one hundred—a fairly typical wedding reception—and it becomes a three-million-to-one certainty that two will have been born on the same day.

The small world of coincidence has shrunk even more than most suppose. There is a slender one chance in 100 that any two strangers are connected by a common acquaintance. But if two more acquaintances are added—friends of friends—it is a nearly certain ninety-nine in 100 likelihood that the two strangers are linked.

Yet the dictates of probability ensure that some of life's most desirable events elude us: Depending on the game, the odds of winning a state-run lotto range from one in two million to one in fourteen million. □

Like malign shadows, vignettes of presidential assassins John Wilkes Booth (far left) and Lee Harvey Oswald lurk behind portraits of their victims, Abraham Lincoln and John F. Kennedy.

Pick a Number . . .

Modern lottery players are engaging in an age-old diversion that was once serious business as well as entertainment. The word *lottery* is derived from the Teutonic word *lot*—a stone, stick, wood chip, or slip of paper that was cast on the ground or drawn to reach a decision. Some of humankind's earliest writings describe the casting of lots to decide whether to wage war, apportion the spoils of war, divide inheritances, assign duties, and determine which criminals would live or die.

Moses divided land among Israel's twelve tribes by choosing lots. Early Christians drew slips of paper to answer vexing questions of theology and settle disputes among the church hierarchy. The women of first-century Teutonic tribes drew lots to decide whether their men should go into battle. Tribal leaders in most early European cultures were also selected by lottery. As recently as the sixteenth century, some English borough officers were chosen by lot. During England's seventeenth-century civil war, criminals were forced to draw lots to determine which would be executed.

The entertainment and fund-raising value of lotteries was recognized as long ago as ancient Rome. During the feast of Saturn, emperors sold tickets to drawings in which the prizes ranged from a toothpick to 100 gold pieces. Royal feasts featured door-prize drawings, not unlike those at twentieth-century potluck suppers. Like governments of today, Rome's emperors used lotteries to fund public works.

In medieval times, lotteries were used by entrepreneurs as sales gimmicks and by governments to fatten their treasuries. Merchants in Italy, Germany, the Netherlands, and England found they could improve profits by selling lottery tickets for "free" merchandise. And then, as now, European towns and villages realized that the games were a painless way of raising revenues without resorting to new taxes. Queen Elizabeth I created the first English lottery to repair the ports of Hastings, Romney, Hythe, Dover, and Sandwich, all of which had been ravaged by storms. The British Museum and London Bridge were both built with lottery funds.

Sometimes, the sponsors of lotteries failed to deliver the promised goods. King Louis XII of France sold more than half a million tickets to pay for construction of a cathedral in Milan in the sixteenth century. The winner would be drawn when the structure was completed. However, the cathedral was not finished until 1805. By then, ticket holders had long since received refunds.

Charity is not altogether neglected in lottery lore. On February 24, 1466, in the Flemish capital of Bruges, the widow of painter Jan van Eyck awarded prizes in a lottery to raise money for the poor. □

41

The Drawing of a Nation

In 1964, New Hampshire became the first American state in modern times to sponsor a public lottery. In opening this door to an important source of civic revenue, the Granite State was following a tradition as old as the nation; public coffers in the United States have long been boosted by the gaming instinct. In fact, the country may owe its very existence to lotteries.

The first game to benefit the New World was held in England to rescue the struggling Virginia colony of Jamestown. Both colonists and the owners of the Virginia Company of London were hard-pressed financially in the winter of 1611. So King James I authorized one or more lotteries—the number was up to the company—and soon tickets were being sold in England with great fanfare. Banners proclaimed the game, public officials promoted it, and publishers took up the cause. There was even a jingle urging British subjects to buy lottery tickets as a patriotic and religious obligation. After all, the message went, the money would help establish a God-fearing colony in the land of savages. The lottery was a great success. By the time of the drawing in the summer of 1612, £8,000 had been raised for Jamestown and £1,000 for the winner, a London tailor named Thomas Sharplisse.

Within a decade, the Virginia Company was earning more from lotteries than from colonization. Soon, however, officers of the company began fighting among themselves over the proceeds. To end the dissension, the House of Commons ended the lottery.

The American colonists themselves, and later the officials of the new United States, made lotteries an important part of American life. In the eighteenth and nineteenth centuries, lottery games built many public schools, endowed major universities, built roads and bridges, settled frontiers, financed wars, and erected churches.

The first lotteries in the New World were private affairs, held to sell property, homes, and goods in a land where hard currency was scarce. In 1719, for example, Joseph Marion held a drawing to sell two brick houses on large lots in Boston's North End. Alexander Kerr, a jeweler in Williamsburg, Virginia, advertised diamonds by lottery in 1737.

Among religious groups, only the Quakers opposed the burgeoning lottery enterprise; at their urging, the Pennsylvania Assembly outlawed lotteries in 1682. However, in 1693 the British Crown nullified this act.

Eventually, most colonies prohibited private lotteries. Although some private operators were known for corruption, morality had little to do with the ban, for the colonies' governors promptly started their own lottery enterprises. In 1750, Rhode Island authorized a lottery to help pay off the debt of Colonel Joseph Pendleton, who had lost an uninsured ship loaded with molasses and rum. The state took a cut of the proceeds, keeping £783 for its treasury.

At one time there were so many lotteries that not even an enthusiastic public could support them. In the years just preceding the Revolutionary War, lotteries were

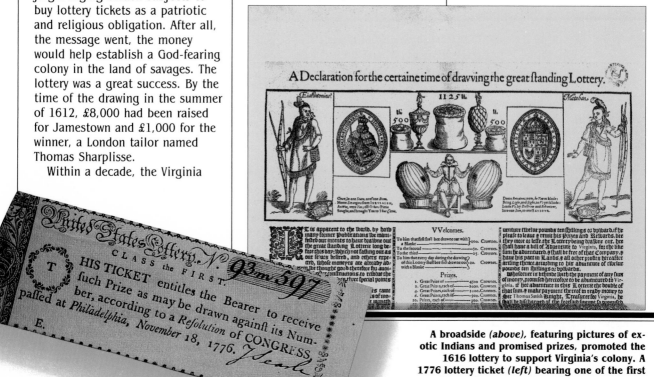

A broadside *(above)*, featuring pictures of exotic Indians and promised prizes, promoted the 1616 lottery to support Virginia's colony. A 1776 lottery ticket *(left)* bearing one of the first written references to the United States helped to finance the American Revolution.

TRANCHE DES PETITS ORPHELINS

LOTERIE NATIONALE

29ᵉ TRANCHE TIRAGE le 28 OCTOBRE
AU PROFIT DU SECOURS NATIONAL

banned by King George. But revolution and war revived the institution. Within months of declaring independence, the Continental Congress enacted a national lottery to raise $1,005,000, with prizes ranging from $20 to $50,000. Winnings of $50 or more came in the form of treasury notes payable after five years at four percent interest—in effect adding money from low-cost loans to the lottery's proceeds to support the struggling nation. The colonies competed with the national game with lotteries of their own.

After the British surrender in 1781, the lottery business boomed, spawning a new industry of brokers and managers, who traded tickets and ran lotteries for a fee. Because each colony—later state—issued its own currency for a time, the early brokers and contractors served as money-exchange banks and investment bankers. Chase Manhattan Bank, today one of the nation's largest commercial banks, started as a lottery brokerage firm.

Welcome missionaries of mammon, the brokers and managers carried the lottery gospel to all corners of the American territories.

Then, in 1860, Louisiana began a lottery so corrupt that its end, in 1888, resulted in federal laws that banned the games until 1964 and still forbid the use of the mails by lottery operators. □

After the Revolutionary War, lotteries built many roads and bridges for the new nation. But they also financed at least one brewery, many churches, and schools and colleges. Two of the academic beneficiaries were Dartmouth and Harvard.

Nice Numbers

Government-sponsored lotteries constitute a $20-billion-a-year business in the United States. Each year, they make "instant millionaires" of perhaps 1,000 people and happy small winners of many more.

But the legal lotteries are, at best, a compromise designed to benefit the general public, not just those who wager on them. Thus, thirty-eight cents out of every dollar stays in state treasuries. It costs twelve cents to operate the games and advertise them. The winners receive about fifty cents out of every dollar bet.

In contrast, Atlantic City's slot machines return eighty-three cents on the dollar, roulette bettors receive seventy-four cents, and habitués of the craps table—a bettor's best buy—eighty-seven cents. Pari-mutuel bettors at racetracks and jai alai frontons share about 80 percent of the dollars wagered.

Few games of chance other than

A plaintive war orphan peers from a poster publicizing the twenty-ninth drawing of the French National Lottery on October 28, 1943. Only a small portion of the benefits was paid out for orphans.

the lottery afford the ordinary player a hope of becoming a millionaire. Even here, though, the payoff is not quite what it seems. A million-dollar winner in the United States never sees one million dollars. Instead, the prize is doled out in annual checks over a period of years. The typical instant millionaire collects $40,000 a year for twenty years—$50,000, or one-twentieth of one million dollars per year, from which $10,000 is taken for taxes.

What is more—or less—this "million-dollar" payout costs the state only about $460,000 at the time of the drawing. That amount, invested in an annuity, earns enough interest to finance the twenty yearly installments. □

Go, Go, Gone

In Britain and Europe, football pools, whose jackpots are related to the outcome of professional soccer games, hold the place that lotteries have captured in the United States. However, unlike American lottery winnings, which are doled out over a number of years, the football-pool prizes are awarded in one lump sum.

Thus, when Vivian Nicholson and her husband, Keith, won £152,319 in one of Britain's football pools in 1961, they were free to spend the entire amount immediately. With Vivian setting the pace, they did, buying clothes, sporting gear, liquor, American luxury cars, trips to Africa and Hollywood, and a house she called the Ponderosa, after the ranch featured in the popular American television show of the time, "Bonanza."

Keith Nicholson was killed in an auto accident in 1965. By 1970, the money was long gone and Vivian Nicholson was working as a stripper for fifty pounds a night. By 1975, she had lost three more husbands; the last died of a drug overdose. Nicholson herself barely survived an overdose of sleeping pills. The one-time pool winner was living on a thirty-three-pound weekly widow's pension, but she was steadfastly trying to strike it rich once again by writing a book about her spendthrift life.

Although the autobiography, *Spend, Spend, Spend,* was a bestseller, its proceeds were not enough to restore the lavish life that Nicholson had briefly enjoyed as a pool winner. □

Eager to begin her spending spree, English football-pool winner Vivian Nicholson kicks up her heels after collecting the winning check.

Big Ideas

On claiming their prizes, most million-dollar lottery winners advertise that the newfound wealth will not change their lives. But when Curtis Sharp, Jr., appeared to collect the first installment of the $5.6 million he won in the New York lottery in 1982, he had his wife on one arm, his fiancée on the other, and a lot of expensive ideas in his head.

Sharp was a forty-four-year-old maintenance supervisor at Bell Laboratories in Murray Hill, New Jersey, when he struck it rich on November 27, 1982. He had already started divorce proceedings against his wife, Barbara, and scheduled a wedding with girlfriend Jackie Bernabela. The winnings established a $50,000-a-year payment for Barbara Sharp and paid for a $75,000 wedding in June.

Sharp's largess continued. He gave $10,000 to his friend Melvin Binford, who had actually bought the winning ticket for him. He bought a $26,000 Cadillac with a $5,000 telephone and a $2,000 security system. Sharp and Bernabela bought a $175,000 home with six bedrooms, four baths, and a spiral staircase.

At last, Sharp settled down and put his free spending behind him—but not before spearheading a drive to aid famine-stricken Ethiopia, to which he donated $15,000 worth of clothes and food. □

Found Money

John Cruz, a retired food-company manager from the Philadelphia suburb of Cherry Hill, New Jersey, frequently buys Pennsylvania lottery tickets. Sometimes he remembers to check the winning numbers against his tickets, and sometimes he forgets. But he never throws the tickets away; instead, he stashes them in a dresser drawer.

One summer day in 1987, Cruz found a twenty-dollar bill while shopping with his wife, Sally, at a shopping mall in Bucks County, Pennsylvania. Then and there, he spent a dollar of his find on a lottery ticket. A sentimental bettor, Cruz selected the couple's birth dates and the number 80, which he also considered lucky. The ticket, like all the others he bought, went into the drawer.

The lottery drawing was held on July 15, and although the jackpot was worth $15.3 million, Cruz forgot to check the results. No winner came forward, and as time passed lottery officials stepped up efforts to find the owner of the jackpot ticket. Newspapers and television stations ran stories about the missing multimillionaire. In May 1988, two men presented what they said was the winning ticket. It turned out to be a clever forgery—one of the conspirators worked for the lottery's computer contractor—and the men were arrested.

In the meantime, a deadline was drawing near. By law, the owner of a winning Pennsylvania lottery ticket has one year to claim his or her winnings. After that, the jackpot reverts to the state treasury. July 15, 1988, was the last day on which the $15.3 million 1987 prize could be claimed.

On that day, John Cruz read a newspaper story—the latest of dozens about the missing winner—and amid the jackpot figures of 01, 06, 08, 10, 18, 22, and 80, he recognized his and his wife's birth dates. Remembering the found twenty-dollar bill and the lottery ticket he had bought with it, Cruz searched through his collection of old tickets until he located the winner.

Later that day, Cruz contacted lottery officials and made arrangements to collect the prize he had rescued at the last minute—an initial payment of $940,000, to be followed by twenty-four annual checks of $470,000 each. ☐

Hot Numbers

Scratch a regular lottery player and find a system for picking winning numbers. Some players take the easy way out and let the lottery game's own computer choose their numbers. Others use numbers uniquely significant to them— birth dates, addresses, telephone numbers, and the like.

There are players who turn to numerologists in the belief that each number has some occult significance. For the price of a four-dollar booklet, purveyors of cosmic insight share their knowledge of what numbers will be "hot" in the months ahead. Dreams, too, are a source of inspiration, and other guides relate their content to numbers. One such guide states that if nosebleeds occur in a dream during 1991, the numbers

532 and 522 will afford a sure win.

Inevitably, lucky numbers sometimes produce big winnings. Judy Nelson, a waitress from Chicago, won $2 million in the Illinois lottery in 1983 by betting the ages of her six children: 02, 20, 21, 23, 24, and 26. On the other hand, Chicago printer Mike Wittkowski won $40 million in the September 1, 1984, Illinois drawing by picking six numbers of no significance at all—and playing them repeatedly for several weeks.

Statisticians—even lottery operators—say no harm can come from using birth dates, dreams, statistics, or any other system. But they add that the hard truth of the matter is that winning combinations turn up entirely randomly. The Ping-Pong balls and computers

that select the jackpot numbers have no memory of past weeks' selections, no knowledge of numerology or birthdays. Nor are they guided by divine intervention.

Only by playing every possible combination of numbers can a bettor guarantee a win, and that technique appears to be a practical impossibility. To be sure of selecting the six winning numbers out of a thirty-six-number pool, a common pick-six bet, a player would have to buy 1,947,792 tickets—a chore that would require placing 278,256 bets every day for a week. Even that effort and expense could produce a loss, no matter how big the payoff: There is no way to prevent another player from also picking the winning combination and sharing the jackpot. □

Profitable Visit

José Caballero is not allowed to live in California, but he is free to collect $70,000 a year from the state. Caballero was working in a furniture store in East San Jose when he won $2 million in the California lottery in 1985.

When he collected his winnings, Caballero disclosed that he had illegally entered the United States from Mexico in 1984. The U.S. government promptly deported Caballero—and withheld 30 percent of his winnings for taxes, rather than the usual 20 percent, because of his foreign residency.

Nevertheless, Caballero's original purpose was accomplished. He had come to the United States to earn money, and he gladly returned to his native Mexico to spend it. □

Star Struck

By most measures, George Magalio lives an ordinary life. He is married to a wife he loves, they have two sons, and Magalio operates a successful business in Flemington, New Jersey, five minutes from his home. But in 1984, Magalio started playing the New York lottery. Six weeks later, his six numbers came up; his share of the pot was $1.8 million.

Then, he says, he started spending seventy-five dollars a week on tickets in New York, Pennsylvania, and New Jersey. Over the next five years, using birthdays and license plates for numerical inspiration, Magalio bought hundreds of tick-ets, and the pace of his winnings picked up.

In December 1989, he won more than $10,000 in the Pennsylvania lottery. On March 26, 1990, Magalio collected a $2.1 million jackpot from New Jersey, and four days later—like a veteran boxer disposing of an upstart challenger—he captured another $1,000.

Magalio's lucky streak is a long one, starting in the early 1970s, when he won $1,000 in a gasoline-company contest. In 1977, he won a new luxury car in a charity raffle.

Statisticians note that, in one sense, Magalio's feats are quite ordinary, for the odds for winning a second jackpot or a third are the same as for capturing the first. □

Winners again, Denise and George Magalio accept the first installment of their $2.1 million New Jersey lottery payoff, a check for $85,985, from acting lottery director Charles Dawson.

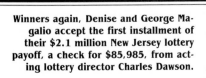

(Easy) Street Person

Donald Sarbaugh was down-and-out in Las Vegas, a victim of gambling fever. At fifty-four, he was divorced, estranged from his sons, homeless, and broke. For six years, he had slept on a pile of newspapers in the recycling plant where he worked. Most of the $150 he earned each week went into the slot machines at the Palace Station and Casino. Then one evening,

Sarbaugh dropped one more coin among the thousands he had played, and his entire life changed.

Sarbaugh's favorite game was Megabucks, a statewide system of casino slot machines that pays off like a lottery. One payday—Friday, February 3, 1989—Sarbaugh had been feeding one-dollar coins into one of Palace Station's Megabucks machines for twenty minutes. He

had already lost $34 when four "wild sevens" appeared in the machine's window. They signified what every gambler prays for, and what Sarbaugh needed more than most, a jackpot—in this case, one worth $2.7 million. Sarbaugh sat down on the floor in front of the slot machine and cried.

He had come to Las Vegas from Lancaster, Pennsylvania, in 1981. Sarbaugh had almost nothing to begin with—only the dream of making the big score. With that finally done, he planned to find an apartment, repay his debts, take a vacation in the Bahamas, and keep his job.

He also swore off gambling. Instead, Sarbaugh told the *Las Vegas Sun*, he would thenceforth play golf, tennis, and other sports—presumably with no side bets. □

Sporting new clothes, a haircut, and a neatly trimmed beard, Donald Sarbaugh (left) collects his prize from casino manager Dick Favero.

Virtue Rewarded

It is said that a little larceny lies in the heart of nearly every person. So it is perhaps understandable that William Murphy, jobless and homeless in Montreal, returned the wallet he picked up on the street but kept the six lottery tickets he found inside. One might be a winner, he thought, good for ten dollars or so.

In fact, just four hours after dropping the wallet in the mail, Murphy learned that one ticket was worth $7,650,267. And it was then that Murphy taught the world the limits of larceny.

Jean-Guy Lavigueur of Montreal lost his wallet on the night of the lottery drawing, Saturday, March 29, 1986. Several days earlier, he had bought six tickets: two for himself and one for each of his three children and his brother-in-law. However, since he kept no record of the ticket numbers, Lavigueur was ignorant of their value.

Murphy, who found the wallet on Sunday, soon did learn the worth of his find, and he decided that the tickets' rightful owner should receive the jackpot. That very night, Murphy presented himself at Lavigueur's door. Unkempt and decidedly suspicious-looking, the English-speaking Murphy tried to explain the purpose of his visit to one of the children, who spoke only French. He was turned away.

Murphy persisted, returning the next night with a bilingual friend. This time, the meaning of the visit was made clear and the overjoyed Lavigueur awarded Murphy one-sixth of the win—$1.275 million. Also sharing the prize were Lavi-gueur, his brother-in-law, and each of his three children.

For Lavigueur as well as Murphy, the jackpot was a godsend. A fifty-one-year-old widower, Lavigueur had lost his job when his employer went out of business. The morning after Murphy's fortunate visit, Lavigueur's first welfare check arrived in the mail.

He returned it. □

With the name of the game emblazoned on the wall behind them, lottery-ticket loser Jean-Guy Lavigueur *(above, left)* and finder William Murphy toast their joint fortune at the Lotto Quebec Office.

THE TINY TOWN of Swampscott, Massachusetts, was $450,000 in the red in 1986, and a new amendment to the state constitution prevented the town from raising taxes. Thereupon Carl Reardon, the part-time commissioner of trust funds, passed the hat at a town meeting, raising enough from citizens to buy the town a $100 ticket in the state's Megabucks jackpot game. The town, like most lottery players, failed to win.

A Slice of the Pie

Phyllis Penzo was a waitress at Sal's Pizzeria in Yonkers, New York, for twenty-four years. During that long tenure, she saw nice customers, difficult customers, generous tippers, and skinflints. But Robert Cunningham, a police detective from nearby Dobbs Ferry, was in a class by himself. Cunningham gave Penzo a tip of $142,857.50 a year for twenty years.

Cunningham, a thirty-year police veteran, was a regular diner at Sal's, where he liked to order linguine with clam sauce and maintain a steady flow of banter with Penzo, other employees, and regular customers. True to his lighthearted style, Cunningham was making a sort of a joke on Friday evening, March 30, 1984, when he offered his favorite waitress an unusual tip: a half-interest in a lottery ticket. Each picked three of the six numbers; Cunningham walked across the street and bought their ticket.

Penzo laughed, then forgot the incident until the next night, when the detective walked into Sal's Pizzeria after work with the winning ticket triumphantly clutched in his hand. It was worth six million dollars: three million for each of them. Cunningham, who ordinarily might have left a couple of dollars on the restaurant table, had no regrets about splitting the prize. After all, he says, Penzo helped pick the winning numbers. □

Handcuffed together in jest, detective Robert Cunningham and waitress Phyllis Penzo pile some of their windfall on a server's tray at Sal's Pizzeria.

Riddle, Riches, and Ruin

Charles Lynn Riddle discovered that a lottery jackpot, far from being a dream come true, can be a living nightmare. Nine years after becoming Michigan's youngest instant millionaire in 1975, at the age of twenty-three, Riddle was sentenced to three years in jail for selling cocaine. The jackpot, he said, "ruined me."

After collecting his first lottery check and buying an expensive automobile, Riddle married an old flame, only to be divorced three years later; it cost him $48,000 in alimony and $175 per week in child support.

Meanwhile, Riddle lost more than $100,000 through unwise investments. Drink and drugs took more of his winnings.

By the time of his drug arrest, Riddle was near the bottom. In jail, which he later called a blessing in disguise, he was placed in a drug and alcohol treatment program. And he continued receiving his yearly lottery checks. □

Losing Winners

No ticket, no prize, no exceptions. Lottery officials are generous only when there is an ironclad claim to the payoff. On May 3, 1983, Mary Molina of Franklin Square, New York, discovered that her claim did not qualify, even though she had the winning ticket. On November 3, 1980, Molina won a New York Lotto drawing worth $166,950. She took the ticket to the vendor for validation and had him mail it to lottery headquarters.

The ticket never reached its destination, and lottery officials refused to honor Molina's claim. They said it was her responsibility to see that the ticket arrived safely. She sued, but a judge sided with the lottery.

Tom Burchell of Peoria, Illinois, lost because of a misprinted ticket. One May day in 1983, Burchell stopped at a neighborhood tavern and bought two tickets in Illinois's instant lottery, Fantasy. Scratching one, the $130-per-week delivery man uncovered three cloverleafs—the symbol of a $100,000 prize. However, Burchell was denied the money when officials discovered that his ticket's serial number was not on the list of winners. The ticket was a misprint. Even so, this story had a happy ending. In a gesture of goodwill, the ticket printer made good the entire amount. □

Winning?

When Raymond Lenox, a thirty-nine-year-old unemployed computer programmer, claimed the $4.4 million Pennsylvania lottery jackpot on September 30, 1983, he asserted that he was indeed a lucky man: He had beaten the odds twice. Just months before the drawing, said Lenox, doctors had proclaimed him free of cancer after a long ordeal in which he underwent several operations.

The announcement made Lenox the media's darling. Stories told how this shy, overweight man had an upbeat attitude, despite his past adversities. The headlines reported on his plans: The lottery checks would introduce excitement into a drab life and buy some luxuries for Lenox and the woman he introduced as his mother. They moved into an expensive penthouse apartment in Philadelphia's trendy Center City. She wore furs. He bought two nightclubs. The businesses would be their security. "I never want to want again," Lenox told reporters.

Within five months of picking up the first $168,452 lottery check, Lenox had spent the money. By the following June, he was once again a news story, but the news was not good: Lenox was charged with writing more than twenty bad checks for a total of more than $100,000. So rapid was his fall—and so pathetic, thought the judges—that Lenox was punished lightly.

However, his troubles were hardly over. Lenox's "mother" sued him for a share of the winnings. The woman, Margaret Lomberk, was actually the sixty-year-old mother of a friend of Lenox's. And, according to the suit, the two had an agreement that they would pool their lottery tickets and winnings.

In 1988 the court agreed, ordering Lenox to split the proceeds. □

Zap

The odds of winning a cool million in the lottery are no better than those of being struck by lightning, yet the lure of instant wealth so dazzles Americans that they ante up more than $20 billion every year for a chance at easy riches.

Some games are easier to win than others. The easiest, except for instant games, are the daily numbers games that many states run. In these, a player selects three or four numbers; to win they must match the numbers in the nightly draw. The odds of selecting three numbers in the order they are drawn—winning the so-called pick-three prize—are one in 1,000, with a $500 payoff. In the four-digit pick-four game, the odds are one in 10,000 and the jackpot is usually $5,000.

The odds are even longer in games with higher jackpots. The pick-six lotteries in Indiana and Virginia use a forty-four-number pool, with winning odds a slender one in seven million. The payoff, however, has been as high as $22 million in Virginia.

Lottery operators have found that fans prefer large payoffs to good odds. Delaware's Lotto has relatively attractive winning odds of one in 593,775, but the payoffs rarely reached $275,000. For big

Catchy names, evocative pictures, and promising numbers adorn a sampling of modern American lottery tickets.

money, Delaware's citizens bet in neighboring Pennsylvania, which promised multimillion-dollar jackpots. Finally, Delaware joined with several other states and the District of Columbia in sponsoring a new high-dollar game with a payoff to match that of the competition. But the odds are correspondingly long, at one in 12,913,583. □

A (Not So) Sure Thing

Until early in 1654, Antoine Gombaud, chevalier de Méré, had been doing well at the gaming tables. Then his luck changed, and the infant science of probability found its first practical application.

One of de Méré's favorite wagers involved four rolls of a single die; to win, he had to roll a six at least once. His purse grew fat, and because of his success, no one would bet him anymore. So, the chevalier changed the game to include a pair of dice. Then he wagered that he would roll a double six within twenty-four tosses. De Méré calculated that he would win the new game two out of three times.

He had many takers, but to his dismay he lost regularly. Unable to find a flaw in his own logic, which reasoned that he should win two-thirds of the time, de Méré wrote for help to his friend Blaise Pascal, one of France's most famous mathematicians. How many throws, de Méré asked, need he make to ensure winning his wager more often than losing it?

Although not a gambler, Pascal was interested in the philosophical and practical problem that is at the core of all wagering—how to make decisions involving uncertain events. He recruited fellow philosopher Pierre de Fermat, and over the four-month period from July to October 1654, the two giants of French mathematics corresponded, each outlining his ideas and commenting on the other's. In the end, Pascal wrote *Traité du Triangle Arithmétique* (Treatise on the Arithmetical Triangle), a land-mark book of probability theory.

Pascal and Fermat found that de Méré was a long way from the two-thirds odds he sought for his game of dice. In fact, Pascal's calculations predicted exactly what was happening: The chevalier's chances of winning were less than even, only forty-nine in 100.

However, Pascal found that he could reverse the odds by adding just one more roll of the dice. De Méré stood a fifty-one in 100 chance of rolling a double six in twenty-five throws.

It is not recorded what the chevalier did with Pascal's advice, but it is reasonably certain that he never got a bet that would give him his desired two-thirds advantage. That game would involve rolling the dice thirty-nine times. □

Mathematical trailblazers Blaise Pascal *(left)* and Pierre de Fermat *(right)* were captured in these contemporary portraits. Pascal's likeness was taken from his death mask.

Odds without Honor

Credit for discovering the laws of probability usually goes to two seventeenth-century French mathematicians, Blaise Pascal and Pierre de Fermat *(page 55)*. But the first successful studies of probability were conducted in the previous century by the Italian scholar Gironimo Cardano, whose work was recognized only in 1663, nearly a century after his death and a decade after Pascal and Fermat advanced their theories.

It was Cardano who first set forth a theory of probability, proposing that the occurrence of supposedly random events was not random at all, but rather occurred with frequencies that could be calculated mathematically. He determined a method for figuring the odds of independent events occurring in a particular order.

Gironimo Cardano was born in 1501, the illegitimate son of a jurist friend of Leonardo da Vinci. The young Cardano was sickly, but he eventually won a medical doctorate in 1526. A true Renaissance man, Cardano fast became the most sought after doctor in Milan, and his renown took him as far as Scotland to treat the archbishop of Edinburgh for asthma. Meanwhile, he also taught mathematics and wrote more than 200 works on medicine, mathematics, physics, philosophy, religion, and music.

Brilliance and versatility could not, however, protect Cardano from misfortune. In 1560, his favorite son poisoned his unfaithful wife and was executed for the crime. Ten years later, the professor was accused of heresy and jailed by the Inquisition; some say his offense was casting Christ's horoscope.

Eventually, Cardano was freed—but prohibited from publishing his works for the rest of his life.

Among his many passions, Cardano held a fondness for dice, backgammon, and card games, and in his last years he turned his formidable mathematical skills to gambling. Earlier than any other known mathematician, Cardano devised the formula to determine the likelihood that an event, such as a particular roll of the dice, will repeat itself. This work resulted in the first calculation of odds as they are used today: a one in ten chance, for example. It is not known whether the professor's mathematics improved his own successes at the gaming tables.

It is certain that Cardano's pioneering efforts were of no help to other gamblers of his time or to Pascal and Fermat, who produced their theories in 1654. Suppressed by the Inquisition, Cardano's treatise *Liber de Ludo Aleae* (The Book on Games of Chance) was not published until 1663, eighty-seven years after his death. □

Numbers Don't Lie—or Do They?

On June 18, 1964, an elderly woman was mugged in San Pedro, California. The attacker, who was described by witnesses as a white woman who wore her blond hair in a ponytail, escaped in a yellow car driven by a black man with a beard and mustache.

Four days after the mugging, acting on a tip, police arrested nineteen-year-old Janet Collins, a white woman who wore her blond hair in a ponytail. Her husband, Malcolm Collins, was a bearded, mustachioed black man. The couple owned a yellow Lincoln.

Although there was nothing else to link the Collinses to the crime, the prosecution believed that it could win a conviction based on the overpowering coincidence of details. As evidence, the prosecutor presented statistics. He assigned a probability to each of the couple's identifying characteristics. One car in ten is yellow, he asserted, so the probability that the couple owned one was one in ten. And so it went: The prosecutor claimed that the odds were one in three that a woman will be blond and one in ten that she will have a ponytail. He told the jury that there was one chance in a thousand that an interracial couple could have driven the car.

When he was done listing what he claimed were the individual odds, the prosecutor multiplied them all together, arriving at the proposition that the Collinses were all but unique in the Los Angeles area. Only one couple in 12 million could match their attributes, he said, concluding that the odds were overwhelming—beyond the shadow of a legal doubt—that the Collinses were guilty of mugging the old woman. The jurors agreed.

The couple appealed their conviction to the California Supreme Court, where Judge Raymond Sullivan painted an altogether different picture of the odds.

"No mathematical equation can prove beyond a reasonable doubt . . . that only one couple possessing the Collinses' distinctive characteristics could be found in the entire Los Angeles area," Judge Sullivan said.

Furthermore, the chance of another Los Angeles couple matching the Collinses' description was not one in 12 million, said Sullivan, but a quite likely forty-one in 100—a figure that cast enough doubt over the original verdict to free the couple. □

Imprisoned by wrong numbers, Malcolm Collins (above) works on a prison forestry project before the courts freed him and his wife, Janet, pictured wearing the ponytail that helped convict them.

Faulty Forecast

In 1944, during the depths of the Second World War, people everywhere asked when the fighting would end. Word spread that there was an answer in portentous parallels found between the lives of five world leaders—Winston Churchill, Adolf Hitler, Benito Mussolini, Franklin Roosevelt, and Joseph Stalin. The correspondences were so striking, some said, that they must open a window to the future.

What the visionaries saw was the number 3,888, obtained by adding the year of each leader's birth, his age, the year he took office, and the number of years he had served in office. What was so striking to some was that the same number came up for each leader. What was more, half of 3,888 is 1,944—certainly, the year in which the war must end. Another division by two yielded 972, purported to be the

precise date and time of cease-fire—the ninth month, seventh day, at 2:00 a.m.

The numbers meant nothing of the sort, of course. Germany surrendered nearly a year later, on May 7, 1945. And skeptics noted that the same calculation, performed with the same milestones in the life of any living person, will yield a number corresponding to twice the current year. □

Contrary to numerologists' assertions, Allies Franklin D. Roosevelt, Joseph Stalin, and Winston Churchill *(left to right in foreground)* had no mystical ties to Benito Mussolini and Adolf Hitler *(background)*.

A Million-to-One Blast

Choir practice at the West Side Baptist Church in Beatrice, Nebraska, always began at 7:20 on Wednesday evening. At 7:25 p.m. on Wednesday, March 1, 1950, an explosion demolished the church. The blast forced a nearby radio station off the air and shattered windows in surrounding homes.

But every one of the choir's fifteen members escaped injury, saved by a fortuitous coincidence: All were late for practice that night. Considering the sanctified site of the explosion, it was not surprising that some attributed the near miss to divine intervention.

They supposed rightly that the odds of unanimous tardiness were slim indeed, especially when the reasons were examined. Car trouble delayed two women. The minister and his wife and daughter were delayed by a dress that needed ironing at the last minute. Others were late because they paused to complete homework, finish a letter, or hear the end of a favorite radio show. One awoke late from a nap. Some could think of no special reason; they were just late.

It is impossible to calculate precise odds for all these events occurring at once. But past performance indicated that each person would be late for practice one time in four—producing a one-in-a-million chance that the entire choir would be late that night. □

Before and after photographs attest to the force of the blast that leveled Beatrice, Nebraska's West Side Baptist Church.

A simple calculation reveals the odds of rolling any specific number from two to twelve with two dice. Subtract the number from seven, ignore the sign, and subtract that result from six. The remainder is the number of chances out of thirty-six that the number will come up. For example, to arrive at the probability of rolling a four, subtract four from seven, leaving three; subtract three from six, leaving three. The odds are three in thirty-six.

Shuffling Along

The shuffling of a deck is as important to a card game as the cards themselves, and every player lives in fear that his hand will be ruined by an inadequate shuffle.

But the question of the number of shuffles needed to create a random deck stumped mathematicians and card sharks for centuries. Little wonder, for a modern fifty-two-card deck can be arranged in a virtually uncountable number of sequences. The number, a ten followed by sixty-eight zeros, is

greater than the number of seconds that have elapsed since the beginning of the universe.

And then, in 1990, mathematicians Persi Diaconis of Harvard University and David Bayer of Columbia University put their minds—and hands—to the task.

The academics played cards and haunted casinos. They even recorded the sounds of card shuffling to help analyze the way the cards were interleaved. They did many calculations and arrived at an answer that they knew was right: Seven shuffles yield a random deck.

However, being modern mathematicians, they employed a supercomputer to confirm their finding. Diaconis and Bayer used the computer to create what they called a hypercube, a three-dimensional picture containing all the possible card arrangements.

To simulate shuffling, they had the computer stretch and fold the hypercube the way a baker kneads bread dough. At each operation, they calculated the probability of each arrangement occurring—and found that after seven stretches the odds were about equal for all combinations.

In other words, seven shuffles will yield a random deck. □

GOOD LUCK, BAD LUCK

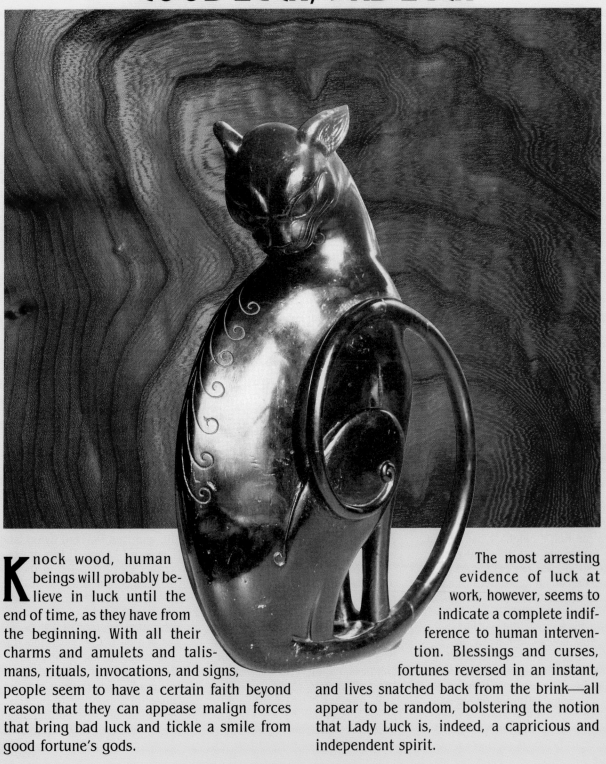

Knock wood, human beings will probably believe in luck until the end of time, as they have from the beginning. With all their charms and amulets and talismans, rituals, invocations, and signs, people seem to have a certain faith beyond reason that they can appease malign forces that bring bad luck and tickle a smile from good fortune's gods.

The most arresting evidence of luck at work, however, seems to indicate a complete indifference to human intervention. Blessings and curses, fortunes reversed in an instant, and lives snatched back from the brink—all appear to be random, bolstering the notion that Lady Luck is, indeed, a capricious and independent spirit.

3

Lucky Leaves

Like so many good-luck charms whose popularity has survived to modern times, the four-leaf clover has a veneer of Christian respectability resting on a substrate of ancient pagan tradition. The four leaves, Christians say, represent the four arms of Christ's cross. Another tradition has it that Eve stooped to retrieve a four-leaf clover as she and Adam were driven out of the Garden of Eden, and she kept it as a memento of paradise lost. Thus such a clover brings the fortunate finder a small portion of paradise. Medieval Christians believed that the plant protected them against witchcraft, the ubiquitous bugaboo of life in the Middle Ages. Moreover, folk medicine in those times utilized the four-leaf clover's presumed powers to

A 1905 French postcard depicting lucky four-leaf clovers bears a "friendship note" from a child to her parents.

purify the blood and heal sores.

Long before the coming of Christ, however, the four-leaf clover was already deemed magical. The Druids of ancient Britain believed that any person owning a four-leaf clover could see demons and, forewarned, could chant the

proper incantation and prevent their mischief.

In the 1950s, science undermined the rarity that had long lent the four-leaf clover much of its power. Researchers developed a clover that always grew four leaves. Again, perhaps, paradise lost. □

Luck at a Glance

In the 1930s, an Italian-born housewife in Boston became convinced that a neighbor had placed a hex on her with the "evil eye." So strong was her belief and deep her despair that the victim finally turned herself into a human torch to escape the affliction.

If the evil eye did not kill the Boston housewife directly, her belief in its powers did—a belief remarkably widespread and ancient. Origins of the superstition are obscure. Some anthropologists speculate that the fear arose in prehistoric times among people who cowered before the gaze of wild

beasts, human enemies, or the specter of jealous gods. Signs of the evil eye occur in artifacts of civilizations dating back 4,000 years. Even today, anthropologists encounter the belief among many peoples—perhaps one-third of the world's cultures.

The evil eye is blamed for a plethora of misfortunes, ranging from crop failure to impotence and death. Prime targets are generally people and things that excite envy—women whose beauty or fertility is coveted by the ill-favored or childless, children themselves, livestock that represents wealth. Still, lore has it that presumed possessors of the evil eye are not necessarily malicious; the malign eye power may be exerted con-

sciously or unconsciously. Some people are merely carriers.

In Italy, such carriers are called *jettatore,* and their ranks have sometimes included the famous and powerful. Popes Pius IX, Leo XIII, and Paul IX, Lord Byron, and Napoleon III were all thought to be carriers. Nor has belief in the evil eye been confined to the obscure. Italian dictator Benito Mussolini was greatly fearful of the power. His butler reported that Il Duce was in a particularly bad mood on a day when he was to meet with King Alfonso XIII of Spain, a man reputed to carry the evil eye. But Mussolini did not avoid the confrontation; he believed that avoiding the curse merely exacerbated the danger. "A person with the evil

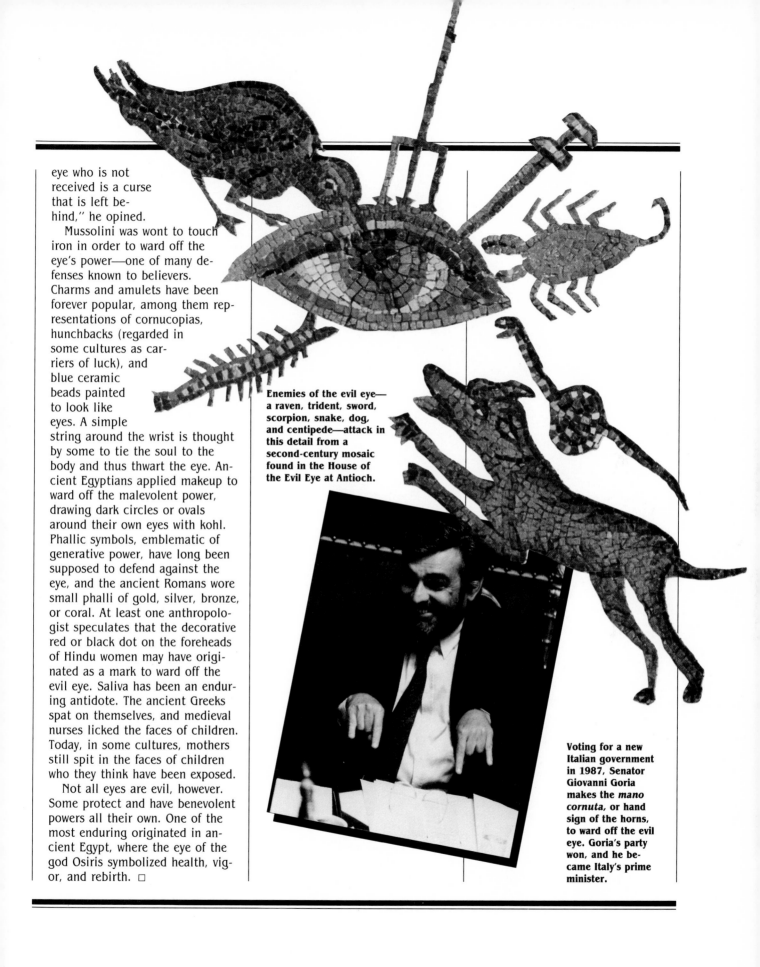

eye who is not received is a curse that is left behind," he opined.

Mussolini was wont to touch iron in order to ward off the eye's power—one of many defenses known to believers. Charms and amulets have been forever popular, among them representations of cornucopias, hunchbacks (regarded in some cultures as carriers of luck), and blue ceramic beads painted to look like eyes. A simple string around the wrist is thought by some to tie the soul to the body and thus thwart the eye. Ancient Egyptians applied makeup to ward off the malevolent power, drawing dark circles or ovals around their own eyes with kohl. Phallic symbols, emblematic of generative power, have long been supposed to defend against the eye, and the ancient Romans wore small phalli of gold, silver, bronze, or coral. At least one anthropologist speculates that the decorative red or black dot on the foreheads of Hindu women may have originated as a mark to ward off the evil eye. Saliva has been an enduring antidote. The ancient Greeks spat on themselves, and medieval nurses licked the faces of children. Today, in some cultures, mothers still spit in the faces of children who they think have been exposed.

Not all eyes are evil, however. Some protect and have benevolent powers all their own. One of the most enduring originated in ancient Egypt, where the eye of the god Osiris symbolized health, vigor, and rebirth. □

Enemies of the evil eye—a raven, trident, sword, scorpion, snake, dog, and centipede—attack in this detail from a second-century mosaic found in the House of the Evil Eye at Antioch.

Voting for a new Italian government in 1987, Senator Giovanni Goria makes the *mano cornuta,* or hand sign of the horns, to ward off the evil eye. Goria's party won, and he became Italy's prime minister.

Sacred to the Egyptian fertility goddess Bast, the cat was venerated in Egypt. This 2,600-year-old bronze cat wears a gold nose ring, gold earrings, and a silver necklace.

Fancier Cats

Throughout most of history, cats of all kinds—black cats, white cats, any cats—have been deemed useful, good, and even holy. The ancient Egyptians revered a fertility goddess named Bast, who was often depicted as having the head of a lioness. The cats kept in her temple were considered deities themselves. Even felines who were less exalted were much loved by the Egyptians. Pet cats were considered members of the family, and their deaths were mourned as deeply as the passing of humans. The animals were sometimes embalmed and placed in valuable mummy cases. While they lived, Egyptian cats were protected from harm by law. In China, Confucius kept a pet cat in 500 BC. Eleven hundred years after Confucius, the prophet Muhammad preached to the Arab world's Islamic faithful while holding a cat.

But all that changed during the superstition-clogged Middle Ages. Belief in witchcraft spread, and people often thought witches could change into black cats. The superstition linking black cats to bad luck probably comes from this time. The "witches" often were just lonely old women who no doubt kept cats for company. But the age of reason was centuries away; old women and young were burned at the stake, and cats—supposed to be witches transformed—were destroyed. In France, there were monthly bonfires on which cats were killed, especially black ones. The grisly practice persisted into the seventeenth century, creating to this day a scarcity of black cats in Europe and England. □

Ah, Ah, Ah . . .

To sophisticates of the twentieth century, sneezing may be an annoying augury of allergy or illness. But to the ancients, the violent, involuntary expulsion of breath was a mystifying phenomenon. In some cultures, it still is.

To the Maori of New Zealand, a sneeze is a breath of good fortune, since, they believe, the creator sneezed life into the first human being. The Zulu of southern Africa regard sneezes as signs of a beneficent spirit.

On the other hand, there is a long and widespread tradition that sneezing is unlucky because it expels breath. For the ancient Hebrews, Greeks, Indians, and Chinese, among others, breath was equated with the soul. To lose it was to die. Sometimes associated with this belief was the notion that violently expelling breath—or soul—by sneezing made room for demons to rush in and possess the sneezer. Of course, such beliefs denote not unreasonable inferences. Death does entail a cessation of breath, and sneezing can certainly denote illness—an obvious connection that was not lost on the ancients.

Whether taken as an omen of good luck or bad, sneezes nearly always merit some response. By Aristotle's time, in the fourth century BC, taking some note of sneezes was already an ancient practice. The usual Greek response was to utter a brief blessing on the sneezer. Later, the Romans were apt to say, "May Jupiter be with thee." A heartfelt "God bless you" became institutionalized in sixth-century Italy, when a sneeze was recognized as a possible precursor of the plague.

But, as Spanish explorer Hernando de Soto discovered when he visited Florida in 1542, the Europeans were not alone in expressing fear and respect for the mighty sneeze. When native chief Guachoya sneezed, his attendants immediately began an elaborate prayer for the sun to bless their leader. The affair prompted the conquering de Soto—in a rare expression of brotherhood—to remark that "all the world is one." □

Passing Through

One need not be especially superstitious to conclude that walking under a ladder can be bad luck—or at least bad judgment. Walking under a ladder can mean being hit by dropped paint cans, tools, debris, or falling workers themselves. But the ladder's reputation as an enemy of fortune far surpasses its logical capacity for destruction.

Some researchers of odd customs believe that the ladder violates a taboo still observed in many societies—among the peoples of Southeast Asia, for example—holding that anything above one's head diminishes one's dignity. Others relate the superstition to the number three—in many places a mystical digit, emblematic of a familial or divine trinity—and the fact that a standing ladder forms a triangle with the wall and floor. Piercing the triangle, a dimensional representation of "threeness," violates its integrity, thereby invoking the wrath of deities from ancient Egypt's Isis and Osiris to the Hindus' Brahma, Vishnu, and Shiva.

There is good news, however, for the hapless passer beneath a ladder. Its evil effects can be undone by making a wish, crossing one's fingers until encountering a dog, or spitting three times through the ladder's rungs. □

Shunning the sidewalk beneath a workman's ladder, New York City pedestrians squeeze between the unlucky obstacle and the Chambers Street subway station.

Shoeing Satan

Legend has it that horseshoes received Christianity's endorsement as good-luck symbols in the tenth century, when Dunstan, who would become archbishop of Canterbury, supposedly endowed the homely iron arch with the power to banish the devil himself.

Dunstan was said to be a blacksmith before becoming a bishop. In his days at the forge, he was rumored to practice supernatural arts—crafts often imputed to smiths in medieval times. One day, the legend goes, a customer approached Dunstan with an unusual request: Would he affix an iron shoe to the customer's own foot? What made the request plausible, if troubling, was that the customer had cloven hoofs instead of feet of flesh. He was, Dunstan concluded, the devil—on hand, no doubt, to tempt the holy smith. Dunstan gave the customer what he wanted but made the job so painful that the devil begged for mercy. He got none. The saint-to-be nailed away and prodded Satan with hot irons to boot, extracting thereby a promise that the Evil One would thenceforth never enter a house that displayed a horseshoe above the doorway.

In fact, by the time the Dunstan-devil deal was consummated, the horseshoe had already been regard-ed as a talisman for centuries. In the fourth century BC, long before Dunstan's time, the Greeks called this spiritual shield a *selene,* or "moon," indicating that the lowly horseshoe was somehow endowed with magical lunar powers. Elsewhere, from Italy to India, the horseshoe's shape has been affiliated with local symbols and gestures used to ward off evil spirits.

If its shape made it lucky, the horseshoe's composition rendered it powerful. Iron, strong and wondrously workable, was so useful to early peoples that they tended to ascribe mystical potency to it. Moreover, it could be worked only by heating with fire, and several early philosophers deemed fire a purifying element, spiritually as well as literally. Such beliefs—and the obvious association with that most lordly and utilitarian of domestic animals, the horse—converged in the Middle Ages of St. Dunstan. Today's horseshoe adds holes to holiness: The more nails a shoe contains, the luckier it is presumed to be. □

A German child sends a mixed message in a 1913 "Happy New Year" card. The horseshoe should bring luck, but holding it with the opening down supposedly allows the luck to run out.

Twelve plus One

At least once every year, and sometimes as often as three times, there is a day of dread, one twenty-four-hour period in which some people find a reason to stay at home, avoiding travel, work, buying and selling, dining out, or making decisions. That dreadful day is Friday the thirteenth, the unluckiest of all days, which has instilled fear into the human heart since ancient times. Friday the thirteenth is a double whammy of superstition, combining two separate and pervasive beliefs in one: a general fear of the number thirteen, and another of Fridays.

Triskaidekaphobia—the fear of thirteen—is a word with Greek roots, and indeed, the ancient Greeks did dread the number. Some scholars think the fear stemmed from the theories of the mathematician and mystic Pythagoras, who, in the sixth century BC, declared that the number twelve embodied perfection. By going twelve one better, Pythagoras implied, thirteen was unstable, imperfect—evil.

It was not in Greece, however, but in northern Europe that the number came to be associated with the day. Freya, the Norse goddess of love, fertility, magic, and the moon had a sacred day—Freya's day, or Friday—and a sacred number—thirteen, corresponding to the number of months in the lunar calendar. When Christians began trying to dislodge the old pagan beliefs and customs, Freya became a prime target of the incoming patriarchal religion. The goddess was reviled as a witch, and her day was marked as evil. In Scandinavia, Friday became known as Witches' Sabbath, and the number thirteen, no longer revered as a sacred symbol, came to be feared and detested.

The mistrust of the number per-sists today. Hotels in Europe and the United States frequently skip the thirteenth floor. There is no Gate 13 at National Airport in Washington, D.C., and many airlines delete the thirteenth row of seats from their planes. Thirteen at dinner is considered by many people to be unlucky. The French avoid the problem by inviting *quatorziemes*—literally, fourteenths—to round out a guest list. The Savoy Hotel of London keeps a large wooden figure of a cat on hand, ready at a moment's notice to occupy the fourteenth chair. In the case of dining, the fear of thirteen is probably related to the fact that there were thirteen in attendance at the last supper of Jesus before his crucifixion.

In America, triskaidekaphobia is perhaps less pronounced than in Europe. The young United States displayed no fear of starting out with thirteen colonies, and defying the jinx continues on the national level today: America's Great Seal decorates the back of every one-dollar bill. The face of the seal displays thirteen stripes in the eagle's shield and thirteen stars above its head. The eagle holds thirteen arrows and an olive branch with thirteen leaves and thirteen berries. The pyramid shown on the seal's reverse contains thirteen tiers of stone. □

Ooops

Spilling salt invites ill fortune, it is thought, and in ancient times it actually was unlucky. It was the equivalent of throwing money away. Salt—essential in retaining water and preserving the chemical balance necessary to life—was so rare and valuable in ancient Rome that soldiers were paid with it. Their portion was called *salarium* after *sal*, the Latin word for "salt," yielding today's word *salary*.

Because it is a preservative, salt was also a symbol of constancy and durability, and therefore of friendship. Thus the spilling of it might betoken treachery or betrayal. Leonardo da Vinci took note of this aspect in painting *The Last Supper*, in which Judas has knocked over the saltcellar.

Like most evil omens, spilling salt has antidotes. Throwing a pinch of the spilled salt over the left shoulder is the most familiar one. Old stories hold that salt tossed in such a way strikes the devil in the eye and prevents him from doing harm. □

Feet's Feats

Midway through the 1951 baseball season, the Cleveland Indians were desperate for success, but prospects looked gloomy. On June 4, the powerful New York Yankees were coming to town, led by pitcher Eddie Lopat, who had defeated the Indians in thirty of their last thirty-six encounters. Against such opposition the Indians, aided by a local newspaper, mustered powerful medicine—15,000 rabbits' feet, which were distributed to fans as they arrived for the fateful game. To be sure that the charm worked, the Indians' management even tried to loose live rabbits on the pitcher's mound just as Lopat finished his warmup throws. The terrified rabbits cowered in their cage; nevertheless, some combination of rabbitry seemed to work. Hexed or not, Lopat did, in fact, yield five runs in the first inning and one in the second be-fore manager Casey Stengel pulled him from the game. The Indians went on to an 8-2 victory.

Although its reputed powers are seldom invoked in so public a fashion, the rabbit's foot is among the world's oldest and most enduring good-luck charms. Its reputation is based on a variety of folk beliefs, some grounded in fact, some not. Superstition specifies that only the hind foot is lucky, perhaps because of the powerful hind legs that up the rabbit's odds for survival by helping it run fast. The animal's burrowing habit contributes to its charmed reputation; because early people feared what might lie beneath the earth, they naturally thought that the rabbit must have a mysterious power over the darkness and evil there.

Rabbits were also thought to have the power to ward off the evil eye, a belief that probably stemmed from the erroneous notion that they are born with their eyes open. Although the distinction was apparently too slight to matter, it is not the rabbit but its cousin the hare that is born open-eyed. It is certainly no fiction, however, that rabbits breed in great numbers, a fact that led to their being associated with plenty and hence with prosperity. The rabbit's foot thus became an amulet ensuring wealth.

In modern times, popular fiction has endowed the rabbit with cunning and wit. From Joel Chandler Harris's wily Brer Rabbit through Beatrix Potter's Peter Rabbit and the hardy rabbit survivors of Richard Adam's *Watership Down*, the image of the invincible rabbit persists. And perhaps any animal so skillful at maintaining a good image for so long must indeed bring luck. □

Wind, Water, Fortune

In 1971, Singapore's Hyatt Regency Hotel was having a spell of bad luck. Its business dwindled while other hotels prospered. To solve the problem, the management called in no high-powered consultants or marketing gurus. Rather, the Hyatt turned to a master in the ancient oriental art of *feng shui* (pronounced fung shway). His prescription for prosperity—successfully implemented—was a redesign of the hotel's facade to discourage unhappy spirits.

Throughout the East—and in a growing number of occidental establishments as well—feng shui guides the placement of walls, furniture, even whole buildings. Feng shui dictates color schemes and landscaping. The purpose: to place the works of humanity in harmony with nature, the better to attract the "cosmic breath," or life force called Qi.

Feng shui literally means "wind and water," for the ancient forces determining health, prosperity, and luck. Its guiding wisdom derives mainly from Daoism, with its notion that the seeming opposites of the cosmos—light and dark, male and female, good and evil—are actually complementary forces, forever in flux, creating balance and unity in the universe. Feng shui masters measure the flow of spiritual energy, determine its strength and direction, and use this information to deflect evil spirits and attract good luck.

In Hong Kong, among other cities in the Orient, a feng-shui master is as important to construction as a surveyor or engineer. Feng shui guides interior designers, who routinely heed its mandate to round off evil-inducing sharp corners and place mirrors where they can help deflect bad luck.

The principles of *feng shui* dictated that China's Great Wall *(above)* follow a route miles longer than otherwise necessary. A Hong Kong shop *(inset)* sells feng-shui items such as red plaques and mirrors to induce good fortune.

The art is not without its Western adherents. After graphic artist Milton Glaser's studio was burglarized six times, he hired a feng shui master to improve his working environment. The new office featured red desk drawers, a fish tank with six black fish, and a black clock to ward off evil. Coincidentally or otherwise, the burglaries stopped. □

Wrapped in Tradition

It was a white satin dressing gown trimmed in feathers—a bit tacky, perhaps, for most women's taste, but doubtless quite glamorous to its owner. Her name was Florence Baum, and she was a chorus member—a "gypsy" in Broadway parlance, one of the questing ranks of singers and dancers who haunt the cattle calls of the Great White Way's casting system for musicals, hoping to sign on with a hit.

In 1950, Baum struck gold, landing a job in the chorus of the megahit musical *Gentlemen Prefer Blondes.* By that time, her satin gown had seen better days, and when another chorus member asked if he could have it to use in a practical joke, Baum turned it over to him. Thus began the legend of the Gypsy Robe, the lucky touchstone for Broadway musicals.

Baum's chorus colleague, dancer Bill Bradley, sent the gown to a friend who was just opening in *Call Me Madam.* The robe, he said, had once belonged to the beautiful chorus girls in impresario Florenz Ziegfeld's fabulous musical revues and would bring good luck to the new show. Starring Ethel Merman, *Call Me Madam* turned out to be a huge success. As a memento, a cabbage rose adornment from one of Merman's costumes was attached to the robe, which was already acquiring a reputation.

Soon it was passed on to yet another dancer in another new musical, *Guys and Dolls.* This show, too, was a triumph, playing 1,200 performances. And the lowly dressing gown found itself in great demand backstage at the opening of every new Broadway musical.

With each new show, chorus members passed on certain rituals along with the robe, rites that became ever more elaborate. It had to go to the senior chorus member and be delivered half an hour before the opening. Wearing the garment, the new owner had to twirl around three times on stage before the show, then submit the robe to all cast members to be touched. She had to visit each dressing room for luck. Cast members of every show were supposed to sign it, and with each new show, a new memento was attached.

Even had it been denim instead of satin, the original Gypsy Robe could not have held up very well under the wear and tear of all the ritual. Full of souvenirs, the much-mended satin gown was retired in 1954, to be replaced by a successor, the first in a line of stand-ins. Each is treated with the same respect enjoyed by the original.

Although the robe has at times graced a chorus member of a Broadway loser, its legend is undimmed. Believers point to many anecdotes to assure skeptics of its magic, including this one: The Gypsy Robe was delivered three days late to a revival of *My Fair Lady,* seemingly a surefire hit. The show closed prematurely. □

Witchworks

William Shakespeare's *Macbeth* is a grisly tale of murder and ambition, a dark drama in which the treacherous protagonist and his wife murder their king in order to assume his crown. It is a play greatly respected by theater folk—but never loved. For 400 years, stage lore has held that disaster dogs the trail of everything associated with *Macbeth.* So firm is the superstition's grip that many thespians will not even say the name of the work, referring to it instead as That Play, the Scottish Play, or the Unmentionable.

Legend has it that the curse of *Macbeth* begins with the three spell-brewing witches whose deceitful prophecies give rise to the title character's fatal ambitions. Shakespeare, it is said, based their dialogue on a real witches' spell, thus rendering the work ill-starred for all time.

On a less mystical note, the play was misbegotten politically. The first production reportedly so offended James I, monarch when *Macbeth* premiered around 1605 at Hampton Court, that he banned all performances of it for five years. James, the first of England's Stuart kings, was the son of Mary, Queen of Scots, who had been executed for treason at the command of Elizabeth I. James was a squeamish soul, and among his chief dreads were assassination, witchcraft, and madness—three themes central to the plot of *Macbeth.*

The first known performance after the ban was in 1610 at Shakespeare's famed Globe Theatre in London. The Globe burned down in 1613, and all the props, scenery, and costumes of *Macbeth* were lost in the fire. Shakespeare died three years later, and the Scottish tragedy vanished from the stage for about half a century. It then resurfaced as a light opera. Music apparently discouraged the curse, which seemed to remain dormant until early in the eighteenth century.

In 1703, *Macbeth* was playing at London's Covent Garden when England was strafed by one of the worst storms in its history. Rains and hurricane-strength winds killed hundreds of seamen, caused extensive damage in London, and nearly destroyed the port town of Bristol. A number of theater-hating moralists of the day proclaimed that the storm expressed God's displeasure with *Macbeth,* whose witchy goings-on were deemed to be particularly objectionable.

During a performance of the play at London's Portugal Street Theatre in 1731, an argument in the audience got so out of hand that a riot erupted and the theater was nearly burned down. In 1808, Covent Garden opened its fall season with a production of *Macbeth.* Within a month, the theater burned to the ground, killing twenty-three people and destroying irreplaceable manuscripts and sheet music.

Mishaps and mayhem continued to haunt the play through the years: Cast members suffered accidents or sickened or died, productions went awry, and even audiences sometimes seemed afflicted by the presumed curse. It was an 1849 production of *Macbeth* at New York's Astor

Sir Laurence Olivier appears as a grotesquely made-up Macbeth in the 1937 Old Vic production of the play that nearly cost him his life.

Place Opera House that ignited a tragic climax to a long-running feud between two actors, England's William Charles Macready and the American Edwin Forrest. At the play's farewell performance, Forrest partisans congealed into a mob outside the opera house. They stoned the theater and smashed windows. The militia, called to quell the riot, fired on the crowd. In the end, at least twenty people were killed and many more injured.

A 1937 production at London's Old Vic theater starred Sir Laurence Olivier and won wide praise, but at considerable cost. Lillian Baylis, manager of the Old Vic, died during rehearsals. Director Michel Saint-Denis and actress Vera Lindsey were injured in an accident. Olivier first lost his voice, then nearly lost his life when a falling stage weight just missed hitting him.

During a production in Oldham, England, ten years later, British actor Harold Norman practiced bits of his title role in his dressing room, careless of the superstition holding that the play must be recited only onstage. In the play's final battle scene, Norman was accidentally stabbed by the actor playing Macbeth's antagonist, Macduff. The wound was fairly slight, but an infection set in, and a month later, Norman died. Shortly thereafter, his infant daughter was accidentally suffocated, and his widow, also a performer, suffered a mental breakdown.

One of the most bizarre misfortunes in *Macbeth's* long and blighted history involved a 1935 New York staging at the Lafayette Theater in Harlem, featuring an all-black cast. It was produced by John Houseman and directed by Orson Welles, and the gifted pair decided to give it a distinctly voodoo flavor, setting it in Haiti and importing some genuine voodoo practitioners to conduct their exotic rites onstage. The production was a huge critical success, with one notable dissenter: Conservative critic Percy Hammond of the *Herald Tribune* called the opening performance a boondoggle and worse. Grim-faced voodooists stayed in the theater overnight, chanting and drumming. The next day, Hammond fell ill. He died soon afterward from pneumonia.

At times, the *Macbeth* curse turns more puckish than malign, as it did for Charlton Heston one evening during an open-air performance in Bermuda. Lady Macbeth was to die by throwing herself over a rampart into the sea below her high-walled castle. The dummy representing the unfortunate lady was hurled to its fate—only to be flopped back onto the stage by an uncooperative wind. The grave moment turned farcical; the audience roared with laughter as a hapless messenger announced to Macbeth, "The Queen is dead, my Lord." □

Broken Legs and Other Blessings

The gravel-voiced actress Tallulah Bankhead was known as much for eccentricity as talent, and among her peculiar rituals was this one, reserved for opening nights: Kneeling in her dressing room before gold-framed photographs of her parents, she crossed her heart and prayed, "Dear God, please don't let me make a fool of myself tonight." She then tossed off a glass of champagne and, thus fortified, was ready for her entrance. Maybe. All might be lost if someone entered the dressing room left foot first. Bankhead would make them leave and then return leading with the right. Once her guests correctly entered, they were likely to spy her lucky rabbit's foot, a gift from her father, so treasured that it was buried with the actress when she died in 1968.

The grand Tallulah was hardly alone among actors and actresses in being almost obsessive about luck, good or bad. In the wildly superstitious world of the theater, colors, clothes, actions, artifacts, and words take on crucial significance as amulets, talismans, fetishes, hexes.

Some superstitions are purely personal. Mrs. Patrick Campbell was a leading star of the London stage at the turn of the century. Even so, by 1939 she was down on her luck and in need of money. Several choice movie roles came her way, including a film production of *Major Barbara,* the stage play written by her friend George Bernard Shaw. She turned it down, to Shaw's great disappointment, because the filming would have separated her from her Pekingese, Moonbeam, a pet she regarded as essential to her luck. ⟳

America's folksy Jimmy Stewart wore, throughout his acting career, the same hat, and John Ford donned a lucky hat to direct films. Comedian Ed Wynne donned the same pair of shoes for every performance. John Wayne carried the same rifle and pistol in all his legendary westerns, and in many of them he insisted on wearing the same clothes and strapping on the same holster.

Stage husband and wife stars Alfred Lunt and Lynn Fontanne arrived at least four hours in advance of every performance, but the English actor Charles Hawtrey was required by superstition to rush in just moments before his entrance.

The theater abounds with more generalized superstitions, some having a firm grounding in reality. Whistling, for example, is strictly forbidden, probably because stagehands once raised and lowered scenery in response to whistle signals from the stage manager. Obviously, a random intrusion could wreak havoc. The color green is anathema in the theater, a superstition probably rooted in the fact that green is a very difficult color to light properly.

One of the most entrenched theatrical taboos is the one forbidding well-wishers from uttering the words "good luck" to an actor or actress before a show. The injunction may stem from the ancient Greek notion that one should conceal true desires from capricious gods, lest they be tempted to thwart such cravings. Thus the proper good wishes—ensuring fortune's blessing and a long run—is the time-honored admonition to "break a leg." □

Tapped Out

In the staid world of professional tennis during the late 1940s and early 1950s, gangling Art Larsen stood out. Larsen, who returned from harrowing World War II army service edgy but unscratched, took to the court boundless stamina and a bewildering array of superstitions and rituals aimed at calming his war-jangled nerves and invoking good luck. His playing style made Larsen the U.S. Open champion in 1950. His habits made him a perennial crowd pleaser and earned him the nickname Tappy.

Larsen claimed that each morning he received a "message"—from whom was never certain—that told him his lucky number for the day. It would always be a single digit, from one to nine. For the rest of the day, Larsen invoked

Tennis champion Tappy Larsen entertains Wimbledon spectators in the 1950s.

Fortune on the Field

Old-time pitching great Christy Mathewson of the New York Giants once called baseball "a child of superstition," and the game's history supports that assessment.

There is, for example, the long-standing notion that bad luck will follow the player who steps on a baseline or foul line while entering or leaving the field. Frank Lucchesi, manager of the Texas Rangers from 1975 to 1977, carried his observance of the rule to a hilarious extreme by frequently hopping, skipping, and jumping over foul lines. Lucchesi's antics earned him the nickname Hippity-Hop. Other players eat chicken before games, touch certain bases, or enter the field on a certain side. Former Baltimore Orioles pitcher Jim Palmer was nicknamed Cakes because he ate pancakes before every game.

But few exercises of ritual have equaled that of third baseman Wade Boggs of the Boston Red Sox. His precisely choreographed movements—from warmup exercises, to a ritual touching of bases and dugout steps, to meditation and the arrangement of articles in the on-deck circle—consume a full five hours before a game begins.

The observance of most baseball superstitions is considered optional—except one: the nearly universal taboo against acknowledging a no-hitter when one is in progress. Violation of the ban, say some, may have cost New York Yankees pitcher Bill Bevens the opportunity to register the first no-hitter in World

Series history in 1947. The Yankees were leading, 2-1, in the final inning of the fourth game of the so-called subway Series between the Yankees and the Brooklyn Dodgers. Bevens was one out away from victory when broadcaster Red Barber, who called the superstition "voodoo," mentioned the record-in-progress during his play-by-play commentary. Seconds later, Dodger Cookie Lavagetto hit a two-run double that won the game and tied the series, 2-2. The Yankees did win the series, four games to three, but Barber was swamped by angry letters.

Nearly seventeen years later, on June 21, 1964, Jim Bunning of the Philadelphia Phillies pitched a perfect game—no hits, no walks, no runs—against the New York Mets, despite deliberately flouting tradition. "Talking about it helped to break the tension," he explained. □

good fortune by tapping out that number on anything that presented itself. During a match, Larsen tapped out his lucky number with his feet, hands, and racket. He tapped the court surface, the baseline, the ball, the net, the umpire's chair. His service was a percussive art: His feet tapped; the ball bounced; his racket tapped; the ball bounced. Again a foot, or perhaps the ball. Finally, he would serve and then wear down his opponent with his tireless energy.

Larsen's habits got him in trouble with fans only once. He had long claimed that, during matches, he talked with a bird that perched on his shoulder. Since nobody could see the bird, nobody objected. Then, at Wimbledon in 1951, a real bird—a sparrow—landed on the court. As the bird stood there, Larsen grew increasingly upset and finally hit a ball at the creature to scare it away. The spectators began to boo, and he was forced to apologize for his uncharacteristically angry behavior. "I thought," he explained later, "that the sparrow was going to attack my bird." □

One-time Baltimore pitching great Jim Palmer takes a break from his pregame pancake-eating ritual.

Rogue Run

Amtrak's Number 88 Silver Meteor route was—and is—one of the line's most traveled, carrying nearly 500 passengers daily between Miami and New York since 1970. Usually, the Silver Meteor is on time and safe. One trip, however, was so plagued by misfortune that Number 88 on that run was labeled a "rogue train."

The trip began ordinarily enough, as the train rolled out of the Miami station with 413 passengers at 9:04 a.m. on August 24, 1983. At 7:40 p.m., outside Savannah, Georgia, the troubles began. At Cox Crossing, eight miles north of the city, the train struck and killed fifty-seven-year-old Mamie Anderson of Savannah, who was fishing from a railroad trestle. The Meteor was delayed more than an hour by the event. Barely under way again, sixteen miles north of the first accident, Number 88

smashed into a pickup truck that had been abandoned on the tracks in Ridgeland, South Carolina.

After a routine change of crews at Florence, South Carolina, the train continued on its way in the small hours of the morning of August 25. Just after entering North Carolina, Number 88 hit a big flatbed truck carrying a crane. Two engines and a passenger car were derailed, and twenty-one people were injured. The remaining passengers were bused to Washington, D.C., while workers at the accident site labored to right the train. The chore took about seven hours, after which an empty Number 88 made its way on to Washington.

Meanwhile, in New York, another train took up the return leg of the

Number 88 run. The jinx followed. Miami-bound, the Silver Meteor hit a car at a grade crossing outside Kenly, North Carolina, fatally injuring the car's driver, Walter Blackmon, Jr., of Henderson, North Carolina. Blackmon, trying to beat the train to the crossing, had driven around the barriers blocking access to the tracks.

Number 88 rolled on, ending its trip without further incident. It reached Miami twenty-two minutes late. The National Transportation Safety Board labeled Number 88 a "rogue train" but exonerated its crews of any wrongdoing in the ill-fated run. An Amtrak spokesperson said the train was the victim of "an incredible coincidental series of occurrences." □

Engine 388 leads Amtrak's southbound Number 88 Silver Meteor into Miami on August 26, 1983, just twenty-two minutes late despite its jinxed run.

Achille's Heel

The Italian ocean liner *Achille Lauro* achieved worldwide notoriety in October of 1985 when she was hijacked by Palestinian terrorists in the Mediterranean Sea near Alexandria, Egypt. The ship's crew and passengers were held hostage, and one disabled American tourist was shot in the head and pushed overboard in his wheelchair. The hijacking was perhaps the most terrifying event ever to occur aboard the *Achille Lauro*, but it was by no means the only misfortune to befall her. The ship had a decades-long history of bad luck.

Construction of the vessel began in 1937 in Vlissingen, Holland. While she was being built, she carried the simple designation Number 214, assigned by her owners, the Rotterdam Lloyd shipping company. On May 17, 1941, when the ship was almost finished, Germany invaded Holland. Not wanting to risk having her confiscated by the enemy, the Dutch owners delayed her completion.

Originally, the ship was to have been named the *Ardjoena*, but by the time she was launched in 1946, she carried another name, the *Willem Ruys*. Already, she had violated a longstanding superstition of the sea, which promises ill fortune to a vessel whose name is changed. The next violation of this taboo occurred after Italian shipping tycoon Achille Lauro bought the ship in 1966 and, the following year, gave her his own name and put her to work ferrying European immigrants to Australia. In 1970, the *Achille Lauro* was removed from the workaday world of shipping, refitted, and turned into a luxury cruise liner.

Then the troubles began. In 1971, the *Achille Lauro* rammed a small Neapolitan fishing boat, causing the death of one man, Vincenzo Chiarini, whose heirs won a 110-million-lire settlement. The next year, arsonists set a serious fire aboard the ship while she was docked in Genoa. In 1975, the liner crashed into the *Yussef Baba*, a small Lebanese cargo ship, in the Dardanelles. No cruise passengers were injured, but four crewmen of the *Yussef Baba* were lost.

In 1976, Italian police seized twenty-nine illegal slot machines aboard the *Achille Lauro*. But the ship entered the 1980s with a far worse disaster: While she was cruising off the Canary Islands in 1981, fire broke out on board. Two passengers were killed when they panicked and jumped overboard.

In 1982, German creditors persuaded Canary Island authorities to hold the ship until claims amounting to $1.15 million were satisfied by Lauro's company. Finally, the liner returned to Italy for refitting in 1983. Less than three months after she was returned to service in the summer of 1985, the Palestinian hijackers seized the ship and killed the wheelchair-bound passenger, Leon Klinghoffer. Shock waves from the incident eventually caused the ruling Italian government coalition to splinter, and Premier Bettino Craxi resigned.

Far from deterring customers, the hijacking seemed to lend the *Achille Lauro* a macabre allure. She was solidly booked during the 1986 cruise season, chartered to ◊

house the judges for the 1987 America's Cup yacht races in Australia, and turned into a floating hotel for soccer fans at the 1990 World Cup games, held in Italy.

Meanwhile, she was living up to her reputation as a jinxed ship. In April 1986, the liner ran aground on a sandbank in the port of Alexandria. Later that year, a cruise was delayed by bomb threats.

By that time, the entire Lauro fleet was mired in financial difficulties. Owner Achille Lauro had died in 1982, and the *Achille Lauro* and six other family-owned ships were put up for auction in 1987. There were no buyers. Later that year, the fleet's administrators were arrested by Italian authorities, who alleged fraud in connection with the bankruptcy declared by Lauro's company.

In 1990, the *Achille Lauro* played herself in a television movie about the 1985 hijacking. One cast member was American Rebecca Schaeffer. The production went without a hitch—but Schaeffer was killed by a deranged fan soon after she returned to the United States.

In January 1991, the *Achille Lauro* was sailing from South Africa en route to Australia, back in the luxury-cruise business. No incidents were reported. □

Devoid of Hope

The fabric of legend sometimes admits the light of truth. So it is with the legendary curse of the Hope diamond. The fabulous blue stone may or may not be cursed, but its history is associated with enough documented bad luck to make one wonder, even if some of the hoarier tales about it hint more at invention than fact.

The legend of the Hope begins in seventeenth-century Mandalay, where a thief is reputed to have pried a large diamond—it weighed 112.5 carats—out of a temple idol. The stone was a deep, flawless blue—one of the rarest colors in diamonds. The act of desecration so angered the temple's deity that, according to the legend, a curse was placed on all of the diamond's future owners.

In 1642, Jean-Baptiste Tavernier, a French trader and traveler bought a large stone that became known as the French blue diamond and later sold it to King Louis XIV. Tavernier is supposed to be the first to suffer from the diamond's curse, having lost his fortune and traveled to Russia, where he was torn apart by wild dogs. The story is, however, disputed; Tavernier's Moscow tomb indicates that he died, intact, at the age of eighty-four. Some say the tale was invented to titillate a later buyer.

In any case, Louis XIV had the diamond recut in 1673 into a stone slightly larger than sixty-seven carats. His successor, Louis XV, had the gem mounted in the Order of the Golden Fleece, an ornament meant to be worn by the king. The ornament was passed along to Louis XVI, who was guillotined in 1793 during the French Revolution *(page 126)*. In fact, however, Louis lost the diamond before he lost his head. All the French crown jewels had been seized by revolutionaries and were

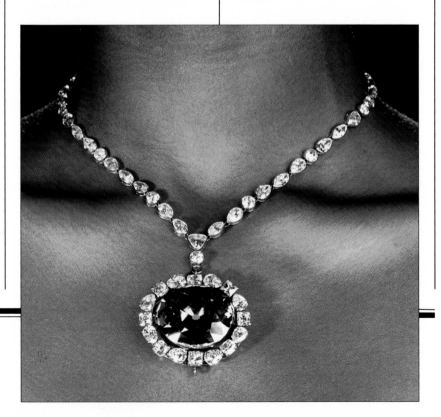

stolen from them in 1792. The French blue disappeared for about twenty years. Somewhere along the line it was apparently cut yet again, this time down to about forty-five and a half carats.

In 1830, London banker Henry Philip Hope bought the diamond that now bears his name—presumably the French blue—from a diamond merchant named Daniel Eliason. The Hope family owned the stone without incident until 1901. Then Lord Francis Hope, needing money to pay gambling debts, sold it to a New York diamond merchant, Joseph Frankel's Sons. Shortly before the diamond went, so did Francis's wife, Lady May Hope, a one-time actress and singer known during her stage days as Madcap May Yohe. She ran off with one of the lord's friends. Domestic malaise was not Francis's only problem. He accidentally shot himself while hunting, and a leg had to be amputated.

The period between 1901 and 1908 apparently was one of manifold misfortune for owners of the Hope. Legend tells that the diamond belonged to a French broker who went mad and committed suicide; a Russian prince who gave it to a Folies Bergère chorine who was shot onstage wearing it; the Turkish sultan Abdul Hamid, who presented it to his wife Subaya—and then stabbed her.

None of these tales has been substantiated; on the other hand, none has been disproved. It is known for certain that the Frankels owned the diamond in 1908. The diamond passed through the hands of several gem collectors before ending up by 1910 in the possession of the famous French jeweler Pierre Cartier.

The stone traveled to the United States in 1911, purchased from Cartier by Washington's eccentric, flamboyant Evalyn Walsh McLean, heiress to a gold-mining fortune and wife of Edward B. McLean, heir to a newspaper empire that included the *Washington Post*.

The McLeans were young, rich, spoiled, and so afflicted with ill fortune that they—perhaps more than all the diamond's earlier owners—are responsible for the Hope diamond's bad reputation.

The ostentatious Evalyn felt that bad-luck objects brought her luck. Accordingly, she regarded the Hope as her lucky charm. She customarily wore it as a pendant surrounded by sixteen smaller diamonds and suspended from a necklace embellished with forty-six more. Along with it, she sometimes wore on a diamond-studded platinum chain the Star of the East, a white diamond of almost ninety-five carats. The celebrated gems glistened from almost every photograph of the young matron.

Punctuating her extravagance with nonchalance, Evalyn let her son Jock use the Hope pendant as a teething ring. When the infant was not gnawing on it, the family's Great Dane pranced through the McLean mansion wearing it. Moreover, Evalyn loaned the diamond to a World War II bride, thinking it did double duty as something borrowed, something blue.

The insouciant McLeans, however, did not escape the bane that went with the beauty of the Hope. Their firstborn son, Vinson, was struck and killed by a car in front of the McLean home. Edward left Evalyn for another woman, became an alcoholic, was declared insane, and finally died in a mental insti-

tution. In 1946, the McLeans' only daughter—who had worn the Hope at her wedding—took a fatal overdose of sleeping pills. Then a year later, the grieving Evalyn herself died of pneumonia.

All of Evalyn Walsh McLean's jewels, including the Hope diamond, were sold after her death to New York jeweler Harry Winston. In 1958, Winston donated the Hope to the Smithsonian Institution as the start of a national jewel collection. The most popular of all the Smithsonian's exhibits, it is viewed by millions of people each year—admirers drawn not only to its splendor but also, perhaps, to the tinge of tragedy lying deep in its cerulean depths. □

Bouncing Checks

On March 11, 1977, Vincent Leon Johnson broke into the home of Nancy Hart and David Conner in Austin, Texas. He stole two television sets and checkbooks belonging to both Hart and Conner. Johnson then decided to parlay the proceeds of his burglary by cashing one of the purloined checks at a nearby office of the Republic National Bank. He made out a check to Hart for $200, drawn on Conner's account, and presented it—with one of Hart's deposit tickets—to the teller. Deposit half to the account, he said, and return the rest in cash. It was a plausible transaction and a sound plan that reckoned without one small difficulty: The teller was Nancy Hart. Johnson went to jail. □

Samuel Ettipio is embraced by fiancée Cindy Henderson moments before he begins serving the prison sentence he nearly avoided.

Lucky Aisles

What Lady Luck gives, she can take back in an instant. An instant to Samuel Joseph Ettipio of Houston, Texas, could be defined as the time it takes to turn the corner in a supermarket aisle.

In the summer of 1989, Texas district court judge Lupe Salinas sentenced Ettipio to twenty-two years in prison for possession of cocaine. But a computer error put Ettipio back on the street that afternoon. He took his freedom and made for his old neighborhood.

It was not far enough, for four months later, Ettipio was browsing through the poultry section of a Houston supermarket when he ran into Judge Salinas. Although the judge had seen nearly 500 defendants since sentencing Ettipio, he recognized the man he had sentenced and promptly issued an arrest warrant.

Samuel Ettipio surrendered to the court the next day and began serving the jail sentence that he had almost escaped. □

Wrong Number

Just after midnight on November 20, 1986, Kansas City, Missouri, policeman Daniel Sweetwood and two other officers followed up on a 911 call. The emergency dispatcher had given the officers the address, which was traceable by computer, but was unable to describe the problem; the caller had hung up as soon as the 911 operator answered the telephone.

As it turned out, the officers discovered at the address a stash of drugs and money and two guns. Arrested were two women alleged to be drug couriers.

The ring members had called the cops on themselves. They had tried to dial the digits 921, the start of the phone number for their leader, and had reached instead the police emergency number. □

David Goodhall lunched in a pub one November day in 1978, had a few drinks, and decided to while away the afternoon shoplifting. He should have thought it through. He strolled into the Barnsley branch of the British Home Stores, boosted a pair of curtains, and headed for the exit. In short order, he was surrounded by no fewer than eight store detectives. Alas for Goodhall, the Barnsley store was hosting a gathering of security experts.

Alfie's Ordeal

Alfie Hinds was no choirboy. His father and his mother had served prison terms, and in his youth he carried on the family's criminal tradition. Jailed for deserting the British Army in 1941, Hinds spent most of his time behind bars until World War II ended. Luckily for him, he soon met a woman who inspired him to go straight. Peg and Alfie married, and he started a successful demolition business with used cars as a sideline.

Hinds's love of a bargain was his undoing. An acquaintance named Tich Martin offered to get him a good carpet cheap, and on a Monday evening in 1953, the two met at a pub to seal the deal. Martin left, supposedly to fetch the carpet, but he never returned.

Miffed, Hinds went home. On the following Sunday, Martin came to see Hinds, not about the carpet but about Martin's car, which he wanted Hinds to buy. They had hardly begun to talk business when Superintendent Herbert Sparks of Scotland Yard appeared. The police suspected that Martin was part of the gang that had just robbed Maples jewelry and furniture store, and Sparks was happy to find four stolen watches in Martin's pockets.

Martin's visit, the watches, and Hinds's criminal past left the superintendent with no doubt whatever that Alfie was one of the robbers. To make the case against him as strong as possible, Sparks persuaded a gang member to incriminate Hinds in exchange for a lighter sentence. Hinds insisted that he and Peg had spent the evening of the crime watching a Gian Carlo Menotti opera on television. A friend backed him up, but the jury did not buy it. Still proclaiming his innocence, he began serving a twelve-year prison term.

With Peg doing his legal legwork in law libraries, Hinds repeatedly sought an appeal, but the courts summarily rejected his applications. He managed to escape from prison three times. During a year-and-a-half-long spell on the outside, he ran a car-exporting business in Ireland. When he stopped paying duty to increase his profits a bit, the Irish police pounced, and he was back in prison.

It took a long time, but at last Hinds's luck began to change. Although prisoners were forbidden to read news reports related to their cases, in 1961 a fellow inmate showed him a newspaper interview in which Superintendent Sparks stated flatly that Hinds had been guilty of the Maples robbery. Under English law, such a statement is protected in a court but not when it appears in print. Hinds instituted a libel suit against Sparks, and after three years of legal maneuvering, he got a court's agreement to hear the case.

In the libel trial, the 1953 criminal proceedings were examined, and support for Hinds's alibi that the police had suppressed now came out. But the biggest break was Sparks's collapse under cross-examination. The former investigator confessed that because he had been so sure of Hinds's guilt, he had improperly denied the man the benefit of the doubt throughout the Maples investigation.

Hinds won his suit, and Sparks was ordered to pay him a handsome amount in damages. The wronged man also wrung from government officials the statement that it appeared that the evidence had not been strong enough to convict him. He did not get the full pardon he felt he deserved, but on July 30, 1964, Alfie Hinds was released from prison. He had served more than eleven years of his twelve-year sentence. □

Briefly free after one escape from prison, Alfie Hinds stands on a street in Boulogne, France, in August of 1958.

Escape to Jail

Two young California men who bungled a burglary nevertheless achieved a certain distinction in the annals of crime: They went to jail even before getting arrested.

Eighteen-year-old Steven Le and an unnamed juvenile accomplice were trying to break into a parked pickup truck in Larkspur, California, on September 27, 1989. Their efforts were interrupted by the truck's owner, who flagged down a passing police car. Cops and victim gave pursuit until the pair escaped by scaling a fence. When they dropped to the ground on the other side, they found themselves on the grounds of San Quentin

Numbers on an aerial photo of San Quentin State Prison mark where thief Stephen Le and his juvenile accomplice unwittingly entered the prison grounds (1) and were caught by San Quentin guards (2 and 3).

State Prison, California's famous maximum security penitentiary. The San Quentin guards turned the pair over to local police. □

Pig Power

The musical toy pig that her mother gave Edith Russell as a token of love and good luck shortly before Russell sailed on the maiden voyage of the ill-fated liner *Titanic* accomplished its purpose. The pig saved Russell's life as she stood trembling with fear and cold on the deck of the rapidly sinking ship.

Russell was among the panicky passengers who flocked toward the liner's few lifeboats after it struck an iceberg in the North Atlantic on April 14, 1912. But there she stalled, clutching her pig, afraid to proceed. Then the pig—with the help of a quick-thinking crewman—took command. The sailor, seeing Russell's plight, grabbed her pig and threw it into the lifeboat. "If you won't save yourself, save your 'baby,'" he cried. Jolted from her paralysis, Russell followed the pig to safety in the boat.

Russell, who was thirty-five at the time, lived to be ninety-eight. Her pig remained a fixture in her life, and she never stopped believing in the powerful good luck it had brought her. □

Titanic **survivor Edith Russell still clutches her lucky pig at the age of ninety-five in April of 1972.**

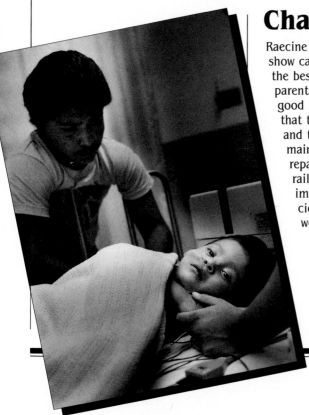

Roy Melton poses with his friend and savior, Lucky, in August of 1987.

Lucky Lucky and Friend

When Roy Melton first moved to East Flatrock, a rural village near Hendersonville, North Carolina, he had a hard time getting past the home of Joyce Harris, a neighbor. Harris's dog, Lucky, barked and growled whenever Melton came into view. In time, however, the man-dog relationship took a decided turn for the better. It happened after Lucky made a break for freedom that almost proved to be terminally unlucky.

A powerfully built mixture of chow and German shepherd, the dog was ordinarily chained in Harris's yard. But one day, stretching her chain to full length, the dog tried to scramble over a chain-link fence into a pasture beyond. The chain was not long enough; Lucky was snatched up short on the fence's far side, where she hung, choking, just off the ground. As if that were not bad enough, the pasture's principal occupant was a bull, and he promptly attacked.

It was neighborly Roy Melton who saved the day. He extricated the strangling dog, gave her water, and comforted her until Harris returned home. Lucky, knowing a friend when she saw one, never barked at her benefactor again.

Three years later, in May of 1986, Lucky returned Melton's life-saving favor—by barking. Melton, now seventy years old, was on his way to the Harris house when he suffered a heart attack and collapsed unobserved in front of it. The dog, who had approached Melton to greet him, began barking furiously, summoning help.

To Melton, the events displayed a proper symmetry: "Lucky is still alive," he remarked after his recovery, "and so am I." □

Charmed Child

Raecine Gomez of Denver could show cats a thing or two about the best way to take a fall. Her parents had been fretting—with good reason, as it turned out—that three months had gone by and the apartment building's maintenance man had still not repaired their broken balcony railing. One day—perhaps on impulse or perhaps after deciding, as two-year-olds are wont, to disregard family rules and regulations—Raecine climbed through the one-foot hole in the railing and plunged three stories to the ground.

An emergency-room physician told the Gomezes that falls such as the one Raecine took without suffering so much as a scratch have a 40 percent mortality rate. To Tillie Gomez, it seemed that a guardian angel had been watching over Raecine, and not for the first time. Two years earlier, on a stormy day in the summer of 1987, Mrs. Gomez had been driving with her baby girl when a tornado struck, rolling the car over three times and smashing it against a storefront. Miraculously, mother and child emerged shaken but unscathed. □

Robert Gomez comforts two-year-old Raecine in the hospital after she cheated death for the second time.

Toddlers on the Track

On May 1, 1989, as their nineteen-car freight train rumbled through Ramsey, New Jersey, and rounded a downhill bend at about twenty-five miles an hour, two trainmen spotted what looked like two bright bundles of clothing on the track some 800 feet ahead. But a moment later the yellow bundle suddenly moved. In that horrifying instant, engineer Richard Campana and conductor Anthony Falzo realized that the train was bearing down on two children.

Campana slammed on the emergency brake and blasted the air horn. The train shuddered and slowed but not enough, Falzo knew, to stop before it hit the children. Running out onto the locomotive's front platform, Falzo shouted at the children—two little boys, he could tell now. They looked up—but they did not move.

In a flash, Falzo sped down the engine's steps and leaped forward onto the track with the split-second timing of the gymnast he had been in high school two decades before. Sprinting just ahead of the train, Falzo dived toward the children, sweeping up a boy with each arm. Clutching his precious burden, he threw himself off the track. The conductor and the boys were flat on the ground, a hairsbreadth from the track, when the wide snowplow attached to the front of the train passed over their bodies. The plow's edge ripped the back of Falzo's vest and snapped the smaller boy's head backward like a rag doll's.

When the train stopped and Falzo could raise his head, the overhang of the second freight car was only inches above him. The injured boy had a gashed chin and forehead, but not the broken neck that Falzo had feared. The second boy was not hurt at all.

Kate Pritchard had just discovered that her three-year-old, Todd, and his eighteen-month-old brother, Scott, were missing from the family's yard when she heard the train horn begin its frantic blowing. She ran to the track behind her house to find her boys with the fearless, fast-acting conductor.

What-ifs followed the incredible rescue. What if a different conductor—one not a former gymnast—had been aboard? What if Scott and Todd had been wearing dark clothes that Campana and Falzo would not have noticed so quickly? What if the track's shoulder had been higher, leaving insufficient room for the plow to clear Falzo and the boys? And what if the boys had wandered onto the track a few minutes earlier, when a high-speed commuter train was approaching the downhill bend? Not even a Falzo would have had a prayer of saving them from its wheels. □

Agile rescuer Anthony Falzo holds three-year-old Todd Pritchard. The boys' mother, Kate, holds Scott.

Cynthia Guerrero stands in the back of her family's pickup truck with the lucky Garfield doll that saved her life in September of 1989.

Saved by the Belly

The Corpus Christi evening sky was still light when Jesus Guerrero climbed into his pickup truck and headed off for church with his five-year-old daughter, Cynthia, beside him. As he was turning into Cheyenne Street, a loud noise ripped through the cab, and a split second later the girl began to scream. Wrenching his eyes toward her, Guerrero was horrified to see blood covering the left side of her face.

Guerrero sped to the hospital, where the emergency-room staff discovered, within a network of cuts and embedded bits of glass, the trace of a bullet fragment on Cynthia's forehead.

Summoned by Guerrero to the hospital, police sergeant John Priest noted an inch-wide hole in the pickup's rear window near a suction-footed figure of the famous lasagna-loving fat cat, Garfield. On the pickup's floor he found a bullet fragment, and a second search by crime technicians turned up more fragments, apparently from a .22-caliber bullet.

Police could not determine where the bullet came from, but Priest surmised that after smashing through the window, it hit Garfield's chubby lower body. The encounter changed the bullet's trajectory, and instead of making a more direct and more dangerous hit, it barely grazed Cynthia's forehead. Garfield, it seems, was the inadvertent hero of the day. □

The Secret Weapon of Mrs. Watts

There is almost nothing good to say about a tightly laced corset. From Paris boulevards to America's frontier backwaters, Victorian women displaced their internal organs with the fashionable torture device and struggled in vain for a deep breath. However, the corset of a certain Mrs. Watts of Linnville, Texas, redeemed its kind when it performed services remarkable for an item of underwear.

On August 8, 1840, after scalping their way across south Texas, Buffalo Hump and his 500 ◊

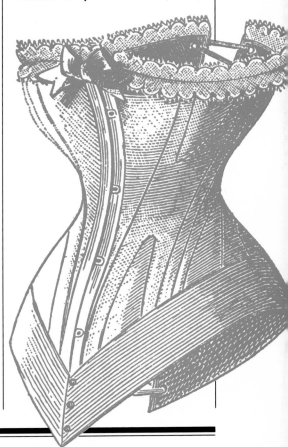

Comanche warriors galloped into Linnville, a port on Lavaca Bay. One of their first victims was Major Watts, the customs collector. Turning to the attractive Mrs. Watts, several warriors tore off her dress, then tackled her corset. After a lengthy struggle with its multiple hooks and crisscrossed laces, the men abandoned the assault but not Mrs. Watts. With her in tow, they advanced to the town's center. It was empty. The residents had seized the opportunity to flee in their boats to the middle of Lavaca Bay while the Comanches were fighting their losing battle with the corset.

After looting a warehouse and setting fire to houses, the Indians turned to their last piece of business in town. Tying the still-corseted Mrs. Watts to a tree, they administered the *coup de grâce*— an arrow shot into her chest—and left her for dead.

When the Texas Rangers following in Buffalo Hump's tracks found Mrs. Watts on August 9, she was not dead, only sunburned. The arrow had struck a tough whalebone stay, thus losing so much force that the injury to Mrs. Watts's breast was minor. No one could doubt that this corset was made of the right stuff. □

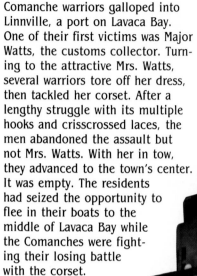

A Miracle on Thirty-Fourth Street

Being alone and broke in New York City is a miserable experience, especially at Christmastime. In December of 1977, luck seemed to have run out on Hawaiian artist Thomas Helms. He had come to the city to find work, but nothing materialized, and his cash was disappearing so fast that he had taken to sleeping in subways.

Around 7:00 p.m. on December 22, Helms went to the Empire State Building at Fifth Avenue and Thirty-Fourth Street and bought a ticket to the observation deck on the eighty-sixth floor. Avoiding detection by the security guard, Helms scaled the eight-foot spiked steel fence surrounding the deck and jumped.

In an eighty-fifth-floor transmitter room, some twenty feet below, a television engineer thought he was alone—until he felt a tap on his shoulder and spun around to see a groggy young man in torn, bloody jeans. A stiff wind had foiled Helms's suicide attempt, blowing him back onto a ledge two and a half feet wide. Knocked unconscious, Helms lay there for a perilous half-hour, then came to and crawled through the transmitter room's window.

Helms's story was told in the *New York Times;* he was inundated by offers of jobs and shelter. But whether he celebrated his seemingly miraculous survival by accepting another chance at life is a mystery. After the story appeared, Helms dropped from public view far more thoroughly than he had dropped from the Empire State Building. □

On Thin Ice

Two young girls from Westbrook, Connecticut, had coincidence, heroes, heroines, and a primitive physical reflex working for them on February 20, 1987. If a single factor had failed them, the day would probably have been their last.

Six-year-old Brittney Blye and nine-year-old Tara Turchetti had gone to buy themselves a mid-afternoon treat. As they headed home with their candy bars, they spied a ball on the icy surface of Salt Island Pond, which was often peppered with hockey players but was deserted just then. Wiggling through a gap in the fence beside the road, Tara ran ahead of Brittney—and in a moment was screaming for help as the ice gave way under her.

Brittney rushed to rescue her friend, only to tumble into the thirty-one-degree-Fahrenheit water, which sent the girls'

body temperatures plummeting.

Although she did not consciously identify it as a scream, something prompted seventy-eight-year-old Jeva Rutkis to set aside her crocheting and go to her kitchen window overlooking Salt Island Pond. Catching sight of the girls' desperately waving arms and now hearing their unmistakable cries of terror, Mrs. Rutkis snatched up the telephone and dialed 911. She worried that the dispatcher would not understand her thick Latvian accent, but the perfect person answered: a woman whose mother-in-law had the same accent.

Mrs. Rutkis rushed out to the pond, and moments later, state trooper Rich Wardell drove up, siren shrieking. When he heard the dispatcher's alert, he had been just a half-mile from Salt Island Pond, on his way to work. A change in routine that day accounted for his being so near; he had taken a road through town instead of his habitual turnpike route. Wardell leaped from his cruiser and scanned the pond. By this time, Tara, in the grip of hypothermia, had sunk six feet to the pond's bottom while Brittney, buoyed by her parka, floated facedown. Spotting Britt-

Brittney Blye returns to coloring books after her miraculous rescue from the icy waters of Salt Island Pond.

ney's purple parka twenty feet from shore, Trooper Wardell took a great leap and landed in chest-deep water. First wading, then swimming, he grabbed the unconscious girl, fought his way to shore and handed her over to two new arrivals, volunteer fireman Pat Murphy and Trooper Scott Martin. Martin's check for breath and pulse was negative. She was clinically dead, but four minutes of CPR brought her back, coughing and crying.

Plunging into the pond again, Wardell dove for Tara until hypothermia forced him to quit. Scuba instructor Mark Hoberman now took over the search. His bad case of flu was another piece of good luck for the girls: Hoberman had been recuperating at home, just a few miles away, when he was summoned to the pond.

The water was so murky that Hoberman had to search by groping. On his third dive, he touched something that he thought at first was a stick. It was Tara's hand—cold, stiff, and apparently lifeless after fifteen minutes underwater.

The moment that the girls were rushed into the Shoreline Clinic could not have been more propitious. Twice the usual number of doctors and nurses were there, since the day shift was almost over and the night staff had started to arrive. Although her temperature was only ninety degrees Fahrenheit, Brittney was breathing on her own. But Michael Saxe, the physician heading Tara's team, guessed that there was only one chance in a hundred of resuscitating her. Tara's heart was not beating, and her temperature was eighty degrees Fahrenheit. The team was not ready to abandon hope, however. For twenty minutes, the medical workers tried every stratagem to get Tara's heart going. The last one—injecting the stimulant epinephrine directly into the heart—paid off. After forty-five minutes of clinical death, Tara once again had a functioning heart.

Many people saved the girls, but so did the mammalian diving reflex, which is triggered when the body is immersed in cold water. The blood circulating in the arms, legs, and digestive system is redirected to the body's most critical organs—brain, heart, and kidneys. The stepped-up flow of chilled blood cools the organs rapidly and reduces their need for oxygen. According to Dr. Saxe, Tara would have died after fifteen minutes in warm water, and Brittney's brain might have suffered permanent damage.

Scarcely slowed down by her near drowning, Brittney was released from the hospital the following day, went home, and climbed a tree. By May, Tara too was back in school but, unlike her friend Brittney, she could remember nothing of their accident, not even the first crackling of the pond ice underfoot. □

LOST AND FOUND

Loss is certain in an imperfect world. Treasured possessions are lost, and the fruits of loving labor somehow slip from their creators' grasp. Adored pets disappear. Great works vanish—a painting, a trove of letters, a journal. Families are separated, brother from sister, mother from son—tragic events whose consequences are seldom reversed.

But misfortune itself is also flawed. Once in a while, what was missing is restored by an idle remark, a ray of light falling at an unexpected angle, a fleeting vision, or a fresh insight. It is as though fate occasionally reverses a loss to make amends for random cruelties.

4

Return from the Dead

Paul Daniluk was an only child who grew up without a mother. As a boy in Brooklyn during the 1920s and 1930s, Paul sometimes asked his father what had happened to her, and he always received the same answer: She had died in a fire that destroyed the family home, and the subject was not to be discussed any further.

Nevertheless, Paul was told about other events in his family's history. His father, Anton Daniluk, had emigrated from Russia in 1914. As a boy, Anton had watched soldiers burn his village to the ground. He had hidden in the mud for two days before heading west. Eventually, he stowed away on a freighter bound for Canada and, once there, made his way to the United States.

Paul's mother, Agnes Dutcheck, had emigrated from Poland. Agnes and Anton met in New York City, married, and in time bought a dairy farm in Homer, New York. Paul spent his first few years there, until the fire destroyed their home, and Paul and his father moved to New York City. Paul later married, had six sons and a daughter of his own, and settled in Denver.

Throughout his life, Paul was burdened by unanswered questions about his mother, and he was haunted by an enigmatic, recurring nightmare that seemed to have something to do with her. In the dream was a red-brick building with white trim, high on a hill. Inside the building a woman paced

a hallway, grasping a broom. Her eyes were fixed intently on Paul.

But Paul's mother was dead, said his father. And so the matter rested, uneasily, until several days before Christmas in 1988, when a series of uncanny events changed the lives of Paul and his children.

First, Paul's son Tom, who was spending the holidays with in-laws in Canton, Ohio, called his father with news that he had seen the name Daniluk in the local newspaper. It is a rare name, and Tom thought his father would be interested. Paul was, but the information had an unexpected effect on Tom's sister, Tanya. She decided to find her grandmother's grave so that she could lay flowers on it: It was time for this long-gone woman

to be honored. She enlisted her brother Joe, and they decided that the best way to begin looking would be to locate the hospital where the grandmother had died.

They started by calling the telephone company's information operator in Albany, the first city named in the telephone book's listing of New York area codes. Could the operator tell them what hospitals in the area existed in the 1920s? The operator could not. More questions followed, with the same response. Finally, in a desperate, intuitive stab, Tanya asked the operator if she knew of any hospital occupying a red-brick building with white trim, set on a hill. Surprisingly, the operator did know of one such place—not in Albany, but 125 miles away, in

With son Paul *(right)* and grandson Joe at her side, aged Agnes Daniluk is reunited with her family. Grandchildren Michael, Peter, Philip, Tanya, Richard, and Tom look on.

Binghamton. It was not, however, the kind of hospital in which the victim of a fire would ordinarily be treated. This institution was the Binghamton Psychiatric Center. Nevertheless, it was a lead they had to pursue. Binghamton, after all, was only 45 miles from Homer, where the Daniluks lived at the time of the fire. With growing excitement, Tanya and Joe called the center. Had Agnes Daniluk ever been a patient? they asked. Indeed she had—in fact, she was still there and very much alive.

Two weeks later, on a gray January day in 1989, Paul Daniluk, accompanied by sons Tom and Joe, arrived in Binghamton to meet the woman who they had believed died sixty-three years earlier. By this time, Agnes Daniluk was ninety-five years old, nearly blind, and unresponsive. Still, Paul sat beside her and began repeating the word *mother* over and over, in Russian. Soon, the old woman smiled. Her pulse raced when grandson Tom mentioned the fire of so long ago. Paul, his children, and grandchildren visited Agnes repeatedly, bringing her news and gifts.

Paul and his sons also combed public records in Homer and nearby Cortland, New York. They even located one of the firemen who had fought the blaze that destroyed the Daniluk home. Slowly, they pieced together the tortured Daniluk family history.

The family farmhouse in Homer caught fire on an April night in 1925. Paul's father was out when the blaze started, and by the time he returned to the scene, Agnes had wrapped her sleeping son in a sheet and carried him to safety. Although their home was lost, the Daniluks were safe. But soon af-

ter carrying him from the burning house, Paul's mother fell to the ground unconscious, for no apparent reason. When she awoke forty-eight hours later, Agnes Daniluk began hallucinating; in her visions, all of her family were burning to death. The hallucinations continued, and ten days later Agnes Daniluk was committed to the Binghamton Psychiatric Center, diagnosed as schizophrenic.

Anton Daniluk took Paul to visit Agnes several times, and it was from one of those brief visits that Paul retained the vision of the woman who haunted him. Lacking a home, and apparently persuaded that his wife might never recover, Anton packed up his son and their meager belongings and moved to New York City. Although communication with Agnes ceased and the Daniluk marriage was annulled in the early 1940s, Anton sent small monthly payments to the hospital for thirty years. But for his own reasons, perhaps to spare the boy interminable grieving for a mother who seemed hopelessly mad, Anton told Paul that Agnes had died. And as the boy grew, he questioned the lie only in his dreams.

As her residence at the hospital lengthened, Agnes was adopted by the staff. They took her shopping, bought her Christmas presents, and became her family.

The reunion with her real family was joyful, even though the elderly woman was impaired by sickness and age. At first she seemed barely aware of her family's identities, much less the significance of their presence. But Agnes Daniluk struggled to life once more. One day, as granddaughter Tanya hugged her, the old woman laboriously repeated, over and over, "I love you." □

Learning a Lifetime

John Burch was forty-six years old when he learned he was adopted. The discovery came quite by accident, just hours after his father's funeral. As Burch and his wife sorted through a box of family documents, they found his adoption papers from the Children's Home Society in St. Louis, Missouri.

The revelation shocked Burch. Never in his life had anyone suggested that he was anything other than the natural son of a St. Louis contractor and his wife. However, an even greater surprise was in store: Eleven years later, John Burch learned that he was one of identical triplets.

The revelation resulted from a near tragedy in Burch's life. In 1982, his son, also named John, was stricken with cancer and was sent to Germany to undergo an experimental treatment unavailable in the United States. Wishing to accompany his son, the elder Burch applied for a passport—and to get it he wrote to the Children's Home for a copy of his birth certificate. When the certificate arrived, it proclaimed the truth about his unusual birth.

Ironically, the elder Burch never traveled to Germany. His son recovered, and soon the father began the search that reunited him with his identical brothers after a fifty-seven-year separation. One brother, John Jones, was a campus police lieutenant at the University of California in Berkeley. The other, James Hahn, was an inspector with the Missouri State Highway Department. Burch was the retired owner of a lumber company in ◊

Warren, Arkansas. By pooling their own recollections and those of family and friends, the three men finally reconstructed their origins.

The triplets, who together weighed twenty-one pounds at birth, were born in a Springfield, Missouri, welfare home in 1926. Appealingly displayed side by side in a laundry basket, the three received a wealth of donations—soap, fruit, clothing, flowers, cash, and even three sterling silver name pins to help distinguish each from the others. The triplets' mother had been abandoned by her husband. Unable to support the in-fants, she sent them to the Children's Home Society for adoption at the age of two or three weeks.

Given new names by their adoptive families, the brothers all spent their early years in or near St. Louis. Although none had any knowledge of his siblings, coincidence brought John Jones together with his brothers on two occasions. One afternoon in 1931, Burch's adoptive father, a concrete-construction contractor, and Jones's adoptive father, a plumbing contractor working on the same project, brought their young sons to work. The boys played together for hours, and during the day, a cousin of John Jones's took note of the children's striking resemblance. John's father, not wanting to reveal that his son was adopted, was quick to hush the cousin up.

In 1944, as a college student, Jones met his other brother, James Hahn. This occurred when Jones stopped in a drugstore while passing through Poplar Bluff, Missouri. No sooner had he stepped into the store than the proprietor greeted him warmly—as "Jimmy." James Hahn, it turned out, was a part-time employee of the store

Sister and brother,
Cindy McClellan and
Reece Sloan, dated
before learning they
were related.

and, of course, a dead ringer for John Jones. The druggist was so struck by the resemblance that he called Hahn and his mother to come down and meet Jimmy's look-alike. This they did, and all agreed the boys' similarities were remarkable. Inexplicably, although he had known since he was eight or ten years old that he had identical brothers. John Jones said nothing of the possibility that he and Hahn might be brothers. For some reason, he said nearly fifty years later, it did not occur to him. It did occur to Hahn's adoptive mother, but she chose to disclose nothing about Jimmy's past.

Three years after this incident, the boys' biological mother asked the Children's Home Society to help her locate the triplets. But, because none of her children had asked for information about their mother, Missouri law prevented the society from revealing anything about her sons' whereabouts. The mother died in 1980.

On July 20, 1983, united at last through John Burch's efforts, the brothers met at the Hilton Hotel in Wichita, Kansas. As they talked, the triplets learned that they shared a fear of water, an aversion to heights, and a love for catfish dinners. As children, all learned to tap-dance. All suffered from tinnitus, or ringing in the ears.

For reasons never explained, John Jones—the one brother who had met each of the others previously—broke off contact with his siblings after the reunion. John Burch, James Hahn, and their families have grown ever closer, talking on the telephone every Friday night at seven and even celebrating the brothers' sixty-fifth birthdays together. □

Mismatch Made in Heaven

For their first date, Cindy McClellan and Reece Sloan met in January of 1988 for soft drinks and burgers at a fast-food shop. McClellan was a thirty-eight-year-old nurse living in Winfield, Kansas, and Sloan, thirty-one, was a nightshift worker at the Boeing plant in nearby Wichita. Both were divorced and had children. They had met through a nonprofit matchmaking service and hit it off at once, discovering a common love of movies, dancing, and travel.

As their relationship progressed, they learned that each had been adopted. Sloan said that he had been one of six children of a Liberal, Kansas, trash hauler. After declaring the trashman's home unfit, officials placed two siblings in foster homes, had two others adopted by one family, and Sloan and his brother adopted by another. Sloan's biological father died in 1984, but the son still kept in touch with his five brothers and sisters. McClellan had been raised as an only child and knew nothing about her biological family. However, she intended to find out: Three years earlier, she had hired a private investigator to find her real mother. Nothing had come of the detective's efforts.

McClellan and Sloan continued dating throughout the spring and into early summer. They danced often at a local club called Eddie's Place. They met each other's children. To McClellan they seemed a perfect match. They even seemed to resemble one another.

Then, McClellan's investigator reported progress. Although he had been unable to find her mother, he had gained access to a sealed file revealing much about her origins: Cindy McClellan was the illegitimate child of a man who had another family. She had been named Lucy Kay and was put up for adoption at an early age. The report included a list of her father's legitimate children. One was Reece Sloan. Boyfriend and girlfriend were half-brother and half-sister.

Initial disbelief yielded to resignation after an aunt confirmed the details of the detective's story. The relationship, once so promising and full, was no more; Sloan moved to the Southwest, and McClellan married another man. □

Triplets John Burch, James Hahn, and John Jones *(left to right)* hold a joyful reunion fifty-seven years after they were separated.

Locked Together

Mary Jones and Joyce Lott, both inmates of the Women's Correctional Center in Columbia, South Carolina, were waiting to see the doctor when they met. At the age of twenty-seven, Lott was serving her third stint in the Correctional Center. Jones was two years older, but prison was new to her.

The women became friends, and soon Lott was describing her life growing up with an adoptive family and getting involved with drugs. Jones told how she spent her childhood traveling from town to town with her alcoholic father and living with relatives. At sixteen, Jones had moved out on her own. She, too, had gotten into drugs.

One thing annoyed and puzzled Jones: Many guards claimed she had been here before. But as she saw more and more of Lott, Jones began to understand why. She was being mistaken for Lott. When the women were seen together, they were called twin sisters. Her curiosity aroused by repeated comments about their similarities, Jones began asking Lott questions about her mother and the town of her birth. Before long, it became apparent to the two women that they were, indeed, sisters. Soon, a longtime family friend confirmed their relationship and supplied pieces of the family's history.

When Mary was about three years old, the girls' father, a career soldier, was in the process of divorcing their mother and moving from one military post to another. When he left, the father took Mary and her older brother, Billy, but left one-year-old Joyce with her mother. Unable to support herself and her daughter, the mother sent Joyce to live with neighbors who eventually adopted her and moved to another town.

The women told the story of their fortuitous prison meeting to a reporter, and soon it was on the front page of South Carolina's largest newspaper. But at the time, neither the writer of the article nor the women themselves knew how singularly ironic their story was.

On the day that the newspaper article appeared, a woman read the narrative to a young man named Frank, whom she had adopted some years earlier. Her reason for relating the story: Mary and Joyce were his older half-sisters. Born soon after the family broke up, Frank was adopted within three days of his birth and grew up knowing almost nothing about his biological family.

All three siblings finally met over cigarettes and coffee in 1988. They swapped stories, compared photos, and talked about how their lives had converged. Indeed they had: The site of their reunion was a crowded prison visiting room; like his sisters, Frank Despiau was serving a jail sentence for drug-related crimes. □

Siblings separated in childhood, Joyce Lott *(left)*, Frank Despiau, and Mary Jones are reunited in a South Carolina prison.

Tippy the Traveler

Since eight o'clock that summer morning in 1978, an animal warden's truck had been parked outside the auto-parts store in Amarillo, Texas, where Bob Vogel worked. The vehicle was locked and appeared to be empty. But when he looked inside, Vogel found one tiny, whimpering puppy barely as large as his hand. No food or water had been provided to the dog, so when he left work that evening, Bob Vogel staged a rescue operation. Using a pair of bolt cutters from the store, he cut a padlock that fastened the truck's rear doors, removed the tiny brown-and-white puppy, and took it home.

Vogel and his parents named the dog Tippy. Although no one could say with certainty what her lineage was, the Vogels believed her to be part corgi, a shin-high dog smart and tough enough to herd cattle. Tippy's size and intelligence certainly qualified her. She never exceeded twelve pounds, and she learned a big repertoire of tricks. And she was fearless. She climbed ladders and ran across rooftops. But her favorite pastime was flying. Vogel, a pilot, regularly took her to Tradewinds Airport near Amarillo, where she would race to his 1965 Piper Cherokee, jump onto the wing, then into the seat. Pilot and dog flew many hours together.

When Tippy was seven, she and Bob Vogel moved to Mesa, Arizona. He worked a night shift, and soon both dog and master worked out a routine that suited them. When he

left for work each afternoon, Bob put Tippy in his fenced backyard. While he was at work, the dog squeezed under the fence and roamed the neighborhood. But she always came running when Vogel returned from work at midnight.

One January night in 1986, Tippy was not there to greet him nor was she waiting in the yard. The dog was missing. For weeks, Bob searched for her. He checked the animal pound repeatedly, placed notes in laundromats, and scanned newspaper lost-and-found advertisements. Then, six weeks after her mysterious disappearance, neighborhood children reported seeing her. Vogel found scratch marks on the front door, but he never saw Tippy. Vogel assumed the worst. Several pets in the area had fallen prey to coyotes, and he feared that Tippy, too, had become dinner for a wild canine.

In June 1987, Tippy turned up again—seventeen months and 750 miles from Mesa near one of her favorite old haunts, Amarillo's Tradewinds Airport. She was discovered by Vogel's father as he

Reunited with her master's parents after a 750-mile journey, Tippy rests with Lorrayne and Bob Vogel senior in Amarillo, Texas.

drove to the airport. Tippy—or a ragged little dog remarkably like her—was trotting along the road. When he had caught the scraggly animal and phoned his son, Vogel learned that the disheveled little dog matched Tippy's description perfectly—right down to a scar on her nose, the result of an encounter with an airport cat.

An elated Bob Vogel took his diminutive dog back to Arizona. There—prevented from tunneling under the fence by a layer of freshly poured concrete—she acted timid and frightened for several months, hiding when she heard strange sounds and becoming frantic when left alone. Eventually, however, the dog regained her confidence and cheerful personality. At last report, twelve-year-old Tippy still enjoyed flying. □

Flying Felix

On December 3, 1988, Tom and Janice Kubecki, their four-year-old daughter, Nadine, and the family cat, a female named Felix, boarded a Pan Am flight in Frankfurt for the long journey to their new home in California. Tom Kubecki, a military security official, had been transferred from Germany to Edwards Air Force Base near Los Angeles. All went well until shortly after the plane landed at Los Angeles International Airport. There, the family discovered Felix was gone,

her traveling crate broken. The family could do little but fill out a lost-pet form, complete the journey to their new home, and wait.

Four weeks later, on New Year's Eve, 5,452 miles from Los Angeles at London's Heathrow Airport, two men loading baggage into a Pan Am Boeing 747 spotted a cat darting into a recess in the cavernous cargo hold. Rather than delay the plane's immediate departure, Pan Am officials notified their colleagues at the plane's next stop, Frankfurt. Once again the cat eluded capture. The plane returned to Heathrow, and again the cat hid and the plane departed. The game of feline hide-and-seek was repeated in Washington, D.C., and, for the second time, in Frankfurt. On New Year's Day, 1989, during the aircraft's third stop at Heathrow since the cat was first spotted, the elusive feline was finally captured.

The ragged, emaciated animal had no identification. No one knew where it had come from or how long it had been riding in the hold of the giant airliner. A computer search of lost baggage records and a cable to Pan Am offices around the world revealed no clue. Jane Ford, a Pan Am employee who had helped find the cat, saved it from certain death by offering to adopt it—at a cost of

$1,300 for the six-month quarantine. A plea for help went out to Pan Am employees. Donations soon began arriving.

Meanwhile, in New York, a Pan Am baggage service agent named Phyliss Seskin read about the cat. Since a computer search of lost-baggage records had already failed to turn up its owner, Seskin volunteered to begin a manual search of the forms submitted by passengers who had lost their luggage. Incredibly, among thousands, she found it—Janice Kubecki's claim filed a month earlier in Los Angeles. The phantom cat of Heathrow was indeed the Kubeckis' Felix.

In her four-week odyssey, Felix had flown nearly 180,000 miles and had visited airports in Madrid, Rome, Zurich, Nice, and Paris, in addition to Washington, Frankfurt, and London. Bettering the record of the most foot-weary flight attendant, the cat had logged 370 hours in the air, covering enough miles to fly around the world seven times. No one knew whether Felix had eaten at all during her travels, but officials speculated that she had drunk the water that condensed on the inside of the huge cargo hold.

On January 21, 1989, Felix made one last long-distance flight— eleven hours from Heathrow to Los Angeles. This time a pampered pet flew first class in the lap of Jane Ford and dined on tuna fish and steak. When she disembarked at Los Angeles International Airport, Felix was greeted by an elated Kubecki family and dozens of reporters and photographers. Toasted with champagne, Felix daintily declined the wine herself, although she did appear to enjoy the attendant caviar. □

Relieved and joyful, Janice Kubecki and her daughter, Nadine, embrace frequent flier Felix after the cat's arrival in Los Angeles.

A Treasure among the Cobwebs

For hundreds of years, a fresco decorated the wall of an Augustinian monastery in the central Italian town of Perugia. Its beauties were known only to the monastery's residents for much of that time. In the nineteenth century, a few travel guides mentioned the work, ascribing it to an anonymous student of Perugino, a Renaissance artist of the region. But neither tourists nor art historians paid much attention, and the mentions stopped. It was as if the work itself had vanished.

In fact, it almost had. But in 1987, Professor Filippo Todini of the University of Udine sought it out for possible inclusion in a book on Umbrian painting. Driving to the monastery, he scrambled through the decayed and abandoned buildings. Finally, he came to a cobweb-shrouded, abandoned garage, once an oratory for common prayer. There he found the fresco. It had suffered years of neglect. Dirt, dust, and mold covered it from top to bottom. Moisture had loosened the plaster on which it was painted, rendering parts almost invisible. But the worst disfigurement was deliberate: In the sixteenth century, the high-ceilinged oratory had been cut in half to create two rooms, one on top of the other. The upper half of the fresco survived. The lower part was destroyed when the plaster fell from the walls.

Nevertheless, the remaining portion was magnificent. The figure of Christ dominates the work, with Saint John and Mary Magdalene at his feet. To the side, the fainting Virgin Mother is tended by a number of women. The scene is set against a central Italian landscape of hills, trees, and water.

To Todini, the creator of this work begged to be identified, but the matter would have to await completion of the professor's book. In the meantime, Todini asked a skilled restorer, Marcello Castrichini, to look after the fragile fresco and analyze it. After taking several black-and-white photos of the painting, Todini left.

In 1989, with his scholarly tome completed, Todini returned to the garage in Perugia with Castrichini. Together they studied the fresco and compared its features with works by known Renaissance artists. Like detectives seeking obscure clues to a criminal's habits, the scholars examined the treatment of small figures and sought similarities in the depiction of trees and paths. Laboriously, they picked out details common to the fresco and other works until they linked the garage's painting to an identifiable artist.

Todini concluded that the artist was indeed one of Perugino's students, one of the better ones—Raffaello Sanzio, who was not yet eighteen years old when he completed the fresco. Today, the maker of this long-lost masterpiece is better known to art lovers as the incomparable Raphael. □

The Virgin Mother weeps in a detail from Raphael's 400-year-old fresco *The Crucifixion*, discovered in 1987 on a garage wall in Perugia.

Welcome Revenge

One July morning in 1971, two seventeen-year-old boys bent on adventure were bicycling through San Francisco's Golden Gate Park. On impulse, they decided to break into the Asian Art Museum located in the park. After forcing open a heavy grate, the two teenagers climbed through a basement window into the museum's conservation laboratory. They explored the quiet workshop, filled with exotic artifacts from the Orient. Then, more or less as a lark, they grabbed three statues and left. The works they carried away were a wooden sculpture of a praying woman and a forbidding pair of two-foot-tall, reddish green, gargoylelike clay figures. When the boys returned to their homes, they hid the loot in their families' garages.

The next day, San Francisco and the boys learned from the morning newspapers what had been taken from the museum. The statue of the woman dated from eighteenth- or nineteenth-century Burma—valuable, but not dauntingly so. The clay figures, on the other hand, were priceless. They were ancient Chinese tomb guardians, crafted during the Tang dynasty 1,300 years ago. Totems of animal spirits, the figures were supposed to protect the dead. Only four pairs were known to exist. Police speculated that the theft could have been the work of sophisticated international art thieves.

The two boys, by now thoroughly terrified of the possible consequences of their act, decided to keep silent. Eventually, they sold the small Burmese figure to a vagrant.

But for fifteen years, the two ancient tomb guardians lay hidden. Meanwhile, the young thieves grew up, married, had children, and led ordinary, law-abiding lives.

Fifteen years after the theft, an act of vengeance brought the long-held secret to light. One man was embroiled in a bitter child-custody battle with his ex-wife. In a vindictive rage, the former wife wrote a letter to the San Francisco Police Department offering to lead officers to the hiding place of one of the statues—her ex-in-laws' garage. As promised, the artifact was there, and its discovery led to its twin. Elated museum officials were pleased to find that, except for a few minor chips, the tomb guardians were in good condition.

The vengeful reve-lation was greeted with relief even by the erstwhile thieves. One man admitted that he had feared every knock on the door for fifteen years. And, because the statute of limitations had long ago expired, neither of the men was prosecuted, and police have never revealed their names. □

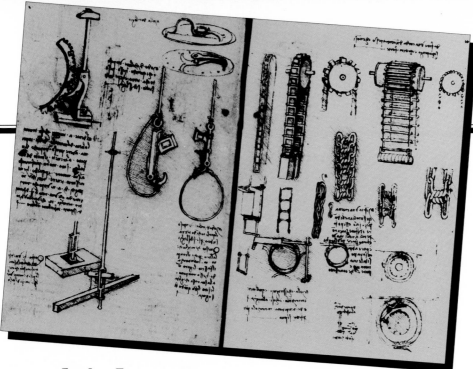

Leonardo's Legacy

During the summer of 1965, American scholar Jules Piccus was researching medieval ballads in Spain's National Library in Madrid when he noticed that several of the library's sequentially numbered catalog cards seemed to be missing. Hoping that the absent cards might represent some long-lost early ballads, Piccus asked the librarian to bring him the volumes corresponding to them.

In due course, the books arrived. However, they consisted not of ballads, but of two volumes of densely written and illustrated manuscripts. The tomes appeared to be the work of none other than the ultimate Italian Renaissance genius, Leonardo da Vinci. Further research confirmed that these were indeed notebooks that had passed from Leonardo to a friend and then to Spain's National Library. The manuscripts had been missing —present in the library but erroneously classified—since the nineteenth century, when the library reorganized its catalog.

The volumes were published at last in 1974, and the world got yet another glimpse into the mind of Leonardo—an artist, engineer, physicist, anatomist, and inventor who anticipated such twentieth-century marvels as the airplane.

The Madrid Codices, as the notebooks came to be called, contain 700 pages, packed with meticulous drawings of mechanical devices, navigational techniques, the flight of birds, works of art, and military structures, accompanied by lengthy notes written in Leonardo's unusual, characteristic script—a mirror image of ordinary handwriting.

The notebooks, reconfirming Leonardo's astonishing grasp of science and technology, are unusual in their execution. While drawings in other Leonardo notebooks tend to be loosely sketched, large, and even unfinished, these drawings appear to have been crafted with elaborate care. Scholars wonder whether the manuscripts, far from being sketchbooks of ideas, were intended to be handbooks on the principles of mechanics.

The discovery of the notebooks solved one mystery surrounding one of Leonardo's most ambitious projects: the construction of *Il Cavallo*, a twenty-three-foot-high bronze equestrian statue commissioned for the tomb of Duke Francesco Sforza but never completed. It is known that Leonardo created a full-size clay model that was destroyed by French soldiers invading Milan in 1500. He planned to cast and erect the monumental work in one piece, but historians had long wondered how he planned to accomplish such a feat. The notebooks provide the answer—a mold, supported and cooled by moist earth, into which 158,000 pounds of molten bronze would be poured. But bronze was appropriated to make cannon for war against the French, and *Il Cavallo* was never cast.

The Madrid Codices increased the world's store of Leonardo's writings by a full 20 percent. And more may remain hidden: The Spanish National Library alone houses approximately 30,000 valuable manuscripts, and as late as 1967, only one-tenth of these had been cataloged. If, as some scholars estimate, Leonardo wrote an additional 20,000 pages of manuscript, more legacies of genius may yet lie undiscovered. □

A Gift from the River

In the southwest corner of Kentucky, not far from where the Ohio and Mississippi rivers meet, the House and Crutcher families shared a home and farmed a stretch of rich bottom land along the Ohio. Although they prospered, luxuries were won by hard work. Then one day, finery floated into their lives.

It happened during the midwinter thaw of 1899. The river flooded the pasture, and Arch House and his brother-in-law, William Crutcher, donned high rubber boots to wade to the rescue of stray cattle or pigs. In a shallow pool that had formed on the river's edge, they found a large wood box that appeared to have recently floated downriver. The crate was too heavy to lift, so the men tied it to a tree and returned the next day with a neighbor, a team of horses, and a wagon. After much muddy work, they wrestled the container to their farmhouse. The carton, they discov-

ered, was packed to the brim with pretty linens, pillows, a pair of yellow porcelain vases, a triple-folding mirror, a silver basket engraved with someone's initials, an ebony clock, a woman's blue-velvet toilet kit, and a collection of books. Many books were inscribed with a name. Some carried dates. But although the goods disclosed tantalizing clues, none displayed an address or other information leading directly to the owner. The Houses and Crutchers left the contents untouched and awaited news that might reveal the box's secret.

Several weeks later, they learned of a boat wreck on the Tennessee River, which empties into the Ohio at Paducah, several miles upstream from the Crutchers and Houses. William Crutcher traveled to Paducah to inquire about the accident but was informed that all of the claims for missing belongings had been paid. When he returned home with that news, the Houses and Crutchers decided to unpack the box. The vases were set out and admired, the clock chimed from the mantel, the books were read, reread, and shelved, and the silver basket, filled with hairpins, decorat-

ed the bedroom of the youngest House daughter.

By the late 1940s, Margaret Crutcher Gibbs, who was seventeen when the crate was found, was caring for the farm and the remaining family members. One evening, as she was listening to a Nashville radio program, Gibbs heard the radio announcer pause to congratulate a Mrs. Lula Webb on her seventy-seventh birthday. The name was familiar, so Gibbs listened carefully as the announcer related that Mrs. Webb lived in Linden, Tennessee. Gibbs ran upstairs and searched the books her brothers had found in the crate years ago. Inside one was Webb's name.

Gibbs wrote to the woman and soon received a reply. Webb had indeed lost a container filled with household goods many years earlier. She and her husband had moved to Colorado just after their wedding, and their belongings—mostly wedding presents—were to follow. But the boat that carried the household goods on the first leg of their journey had hardly gotten under way when it was wrecked, and for fifty years, Webb had assumed that all her beloved belongings rested in the mud at the bottom of the Tennessee River.

Webb—who had returned to live in Tennessee after only two years in Colorado—sent her son to retrieve what was left of her belongings. Several months before her death, she was reunited with her wedding gifts: the ebony clock, which had long since stopped ticking; the lone survivor of a pair of porcelain vases; the folding mirror, now missing a piece of its glass; and the books—dog-eared, well-worn, and well-loved by a large Kentucky family. □

A 1949 newspaper pictures Margaret Crutcher Gibbs as she prepares to return wedding gifts to their owner, fifty years after the Ohio River swept them into her life.

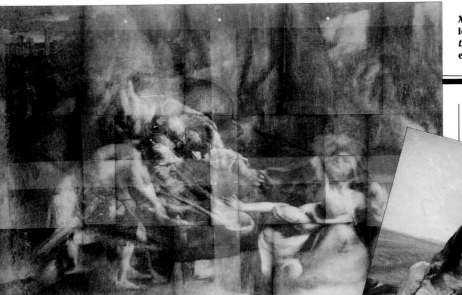

X-rays reveal how Jean-François Millet hid his painting *Captivity of the Jews in Babylon* beneath another work, *Young Shepherdess (inset).*

A Captive Work

At the 1848 Paris Salon, the young painter Jean-François Millet exhibited his most ambitious work yet, *Captivity of the Jews in Babylon.* It was a powerful depiction of Assyrian soldiers ordering defiant, black-veiled women to entertain them. Its biblical theme and grand, dramatic style conformed to the artistic standards of the day. Yet critics judged *Captivity* harshly, complaining that the paint was too heavily applied, and the soldiers were excessively violent. Following its disastrous debut, *Captivity* vanished.

Two years later, Millet exhibited *The Sower*, an eloquent work that helped launch the era of artistic realism—a breakthrough that historians link directly to the modern art of the twentieth century. To artists and students, *Captivity* represented an important link in the transition between eras. Thus for more than 100 years, art scholars searched in vain for the missing work. The artist's colleagues never mentioned having seen it, and even Millet's biographer, who described the painting many years later, had to recall it from memory.

There was the possibility that Millet, stung by *Captivity's* poor reception, simply painted over it. This is common, especially among young, poor artists, who reuse canvas rather than waste it. X-rays were used to look beneath the surfaces of Millet works painted shortly after 1848, but they revealed nothing resembling *Captivity.*

In the spring of 1984—136 years after the first and last showing of *Captivity*—the Boston Museum of Fine Arts began preparing a major Millet exhibition. As workers and curators readied the galleries, one of the artist's most famous later paintings, *Young Shepherdess*, was taken from its normal hangings and set on the floor, leaning against a wall. Seen from this angle, the work exhibited unusual new features. Quite noticeable were bumps and ridges beneath its surface. Expecting to find minor compositional changes made during the painting's creation, curators decided to x-ray it. This had not been done during the search for *Captivity* because *Shepherdess* was finished in the early 1870s, some twenty-two years after *Captivity* disappeared. This was believed to be long after Millet would have needed to save money by reusing a canvas.

But that is what he did. Beneath the later work lay the unmistakable image of *Captivity of the Jews in Babylon.* Historians surmise that Millet stored the much-criticized work in his family's home in Cherbourg. Meanwhile, he lived and worked in Paris. When the Franco-Prussian War erupted in 1870, Millet moved his wife and children to the safety of their country home. Scholars guess that a shortage of canvas in Cherbourg forced Millet to rummage through the attic for supplies. There he found *Captivity*, scraped off much of the old image with a comb, and covered it with a new painting.

Although scholars finally know where *Captivity* resides, they will never view it directly. It has become an inseparable part of the *Shepherdess* and is visible only in shadowy black-and-white images on x-ray film. □

Strings Attached

On the eve of World War I, Josef Totzauer, an eighteen-year-old musician in Königsberg, East Prussia, was shopping for a violin. After examining many instruments, the young man encountered a small, beautifully carved and burnished instrument. A faded inscription said that it had been crafted in 1739 by Johannes Jais, a master Bavarian violinmaker. Totzauer picked up the instrument, tuned it, and found that the violin's sound was as delightful as its appearance: unique, resonant, and wonderfully clear. Within minutes, he had bought the violin and affectionately dubbed it Jaisie.

A few months later, war broke out and Totzauer's promising career—already marked by his appointment as concertmaster and soloist for the Königsberg Opera House—was interrupted. Jaisie was set aside until after the war, when Totzauer began touring the concert halls of Europe and winning praise and recognition wherever he lifted the delicate, golden-hued violin.

On two occasions, Totzauer almost lost his beloved Jaisie. One evening, fumbling for the keys to his apartment, he dropped his violin case. Sickened, he watched as the violin tumbled down four flights of unyielding marble steps. Remarkably, the violin survived the fall intact, with only a couple of minor marks. It still played beautifully. Several months later, as Totzauer was bicycling to practice at the Leipzig Conservatory, the violin case once more slipped from his grasp, falling this time directly into the path of a truck. He opened the case expecting the worst—and found his instrument virtually undamaged. But this time the violin seemed to have lost some of its lovely tone. Before long, the musician replaced his long-used instrument with another—a large French-built violin whose very appearance augured its powerful, dark tones.

Almost immediately, Totzauer knew he had made a mistake. The French violin lacked the sweetness of Jaisie's sound. Totzauer rushed to exchange the instruments, only to learn that the small violin was gone—sold for cash to a stranger from Czechoslovakia.

Nevertheless, the French violin served the young violinist well. In 1922, Totzauer immigrated to the United States, where his reputation grew. He settled in northern New Jersey, and he founded the Paterson Philharmonic Orchestra and operated a music school in Ridgewood. Eventually, the French violin was replaced by a Guarnerius, one of the finest instruments ever made. Still, Totzauer often thought of his favorite, Jaisie.

One day in 1952, Totzauer received a letter from a musician he knew in Nebraska. Years earlier, Totzauer had recommended a certain European dealer as a source for new violins, and it was from this dealer that the Nebraska musician had acquired his most recent instrument. Now the Nebraska colleague was ill; he needed money and had to sell the violin. Would Totzauer buy it? Unable to refuse such a request, Totzauer agreed. He paid no more attention to the matter until the instrument arrived, and he carefully removed it from its wooden crate.

There the violinist found, underneath layers of protective wrapping, a small gem of a violin, its finish glowing in the familiar golden hue of the long-lost Jaisie. □

This handwrought 1739 Jais violin shares the rich colors of Josef Totzauer's beloved Jaisie.

Boswell's Boswells

James Boswell, the Scotsman who so brilliantly recorded the habits, conversations, and views of eighteenth-century London, is regarded as one of history's greatest observers. *The Life of Samuel Johnson*, Boswell's biography of lexicographer and moralist Samuel Johnson, is considered one of the most insightful studies of one person by another in the English language. Inevitably, Boswell's ingenious discourses about others paint a vivid self-portrait of the writer as well. At times it is an unflattering one. The man who was by birth Scotland's Laird of Auchinleck, by training a lawyer, husband to a devoted wife, and father of five children, was also an uninhibited reveler in life's less reputable pleasures. By the age of twenty-one, he had fathered an illegitimate child, and his writings attest to frequent episodes of drink and debauchery.

For this reason, Boswell's own children and grandchildren feared the record of his exploits would be an embarrassment. After Boswell's death, they did their best to obscure and conceal the whereabouts of the piles of unpublished correspondence and journals that he left. So successful were they that, until the middle of the nineteenth century, scholars believed that the bulk of the biographer's private papers had been destroyed.

When Boswell died in 1795, he left the fate of his unpublished papers in the hands of three trustees. One, the Reverend W. J. Temple, died just one year after Boswell. The other two, Sir William Forbes and Edmond Malone, examined the works and decided that they should be left to one

of Boswell's sons. Malone noted at the time that a particular letter had been "burned in a mass of papers"—a phrase that was later viewed by scholars as proof that Boswell's letters and journals had indeed been destroyed.

So the matter rested until a series of uncanny accidents and coincidences brought Boswell's papers back from the ashes. A chance encounter here, a comment there, led to their discovery in bags, boxes, cabinets, and trunks in Ireland, Scotland, and France.

The first serendipitous surfacing of the papers took place in 1840, when a Major Stone of the East India Trading Company purchased an item wrapped in paper from a shop in Boulogne, France. The major noticed that the wrapping

was in fact a letter, signed by none other than James Boswell. He asked whether the shopkeeper had any more such paper and soon found himself in possession of ninety-seven letters written by Boswell to his close friend W. J. Temple. Scholars conjecture that the letters were originally carried to France by Temple's son-in-law, Charles Powlett, who fled to France to escape creditors. Upon Powlett's death in 1834, the papers probably were sent to a rag merchant, who sold them to the shopkeeper.

Eighty years passed. Then, a dart tossed in the darkness surrounding Boswell's works found its mark. In 1920, Chauncey B. Tinker, a Yale University professor with an interest in Boswell placed an advertisement in the *London Times Lit-* ◊

erary Supplement asking readers for information about any of the biographer's writings. He was rewarded with two replies, both directing him to Malahide Castle near Dublin, owned by Lord Talbot de Malahide, the great-great-grandson of James Boswell.

In 1925, Tinker paid his first and only visit to Malahide at the invitation of Lord and Lady Talbot and was shown what no student of the eighteenth century had dreamed of viewing: an ebony cabinet stuffed with Boswell's correspondence and journals. Lord Talbot also described two unopened trunks belonging to Boswell that were stored in the castle. However, Lord Talbot had no intention of parting with the material, and the professor returned to America, awed but empty-handed.

The person who ultimately acquired the Boswell papers was an American collector endowed with an abundance of wit, patience, perseverance, money, and charm. Lieutenant-Colonel Ralph H. Isham, a former Yale student, had served with the British Army during World War I and was familiar with English ways. Carefully and tactfully, he won an invitation to Malahide in July of 1926. On that visit, Isham managed to buy a single Boswell letter for $2,500. Over the next eighteen months, through persuasion, finesse, and an appeal to Lady Talbot's desire for financial security, Isham arranged to purchase the entire collection. The Talbots insisted on the right to censor all distasteful material.

And that was that—until 1930, when two more batches of Boswellia were accidentally discovered. The first emerged at Malahide, hidden in a box of croquet equipment. The second was in Scotland, at Fettercairn House outside Aberdeen, the family seat of descendants of Boswell's trustee Sir William Forbes. Professor C. Colleer Abbott of the University of Aberdeen was researching the eighteenth-century philosopher James Beattie at Fettercairn when he came across Boswell's own *London Journal* and 1,600 of his letters. Apparently, Forbes had died during his examination of the Boswell papers.

As though a literary ghost were deliberately placing them before unsuspecting workers, Boswell's papers continued to come to light at the Talbots' Malahide Castle. And, if a ghost was at work, Colonel Isham was his agent. In 1937, Isham asked to have one more look around Malahide. As fate would have it, he did indeed uncover another long-lost cache of papers that had been overlooked by the Talbots. Naturally, he bought them. In 1940, while cleaning out a stable loft, workers brought down two old boxes filled with more papers. In 1948, upon the death of Lord Talbot, another small hoard was discovered. In every instance, Colonel Isham came forth to buy the papers.

Finally, it was Isham—now nearly bankrupted by his purchases—who consolidated the papers found at Fettercairn. After a ten-year legal struggle, a court had divided them between two groups, each representing one of Boswell's great-granddaughters. Having devoted the better part of his life and savings to the acquisition of the Boswell papers, Colonel Isham sold them to Yale. In 1950, the papers moved to New Haven, where they remain to this day. □

Antiquity Unbound

Frank Mowery's job as a conservator at the Folger Shakespeare Library in Washington, D.C., makes him part craftsman and part detective. The Folger Library houses 250,000 manuscripts, works of art, and rare books from Shakespeare's time. They concern not only theater and literature, but the political, social, and intellectual life of fifteenth- and sixteenth-century England. Frank Mowery is one of those charged with maintaining these volumes and interpreting their significance.

One day in October of 1984, Mowery was rebinding two sixteenth-century medical books that had been badly damaged by mice and insects. Sometime in the past, the two volumes had been bound together as one, so Mowery first carefully separated them, setting aside the material that held the books together. Then he put each in a separate cover.

His repair task completed, Mowery turned his attention to the leftover parts. He knew that bookbinders often took pages of old books—those considered of negligible value—and reused them as binding materials for other volumes deemed more worthy. Thousands of the Folger Library's volumes are no doubt held together by pages of other books.

Thus it was routine for Mowery to examine the material. It turned out to be vellum—sheepskin or calfskin—that had been covered with several layers of paper. This

was not surprising, and slowly, methodically, he stripped the paper from the vellum. Soon there appeared a Latin text. Still no surprise; Latin was commonly used in all sorts of writings for centuries. Mowery continued with his work. Eventually, he finished with a two-page document written in barely decipherable Latin script.

Further investigation revealed that Mowery had found one of the oldest surviving manuscripts from the British Isles—a fragment of a well-known religious text, *Historica Ecclesiastica* (History of the Church), copied by an Irish monk in the seventh century.

The *Historica Ecclesiastica* was originally composed in Greek during the third century but was commonly transcribed into Latin by monks intent on spreading Christi-

anity. The scrap's age was indicated by the type of script—a rare early Irish style called half-uncial that the clergy used during the sixth and seventh centuries.

Mowery and scholar-detectives like him theorize that the seventh-century fragment found its way into a sixteenth-century medical book during that century's Protestant Reformation. The original work, they believe, was carried from Ireland to Northumbria, in northern England, not long after it was transcribed. During the Reformation, when Catholic monasteries were ransacked, books such as *Historica Ecclesiastica* were either destroyed or, as this one had been, salvaged by a thrifty bookbinder. □

Rare Irish script marks the work of seventh-century monks.

A Novel Tale

While living in London in the late 1960s, American author George Feifer wrote *The Girl from Petrovka*, a novel about a Russian girl and an American news correspondent in Moscow. The book was about to be published in England in the autumn of 1971 when Feifer was asked to Americanize it for release in the United States. The task involved changing British spellings and word usages to conform to American style—substituting the American *color* for the British *colour*, *subway* for *underground*, or *elevator* for *lift*, for example. Page by page, hour after hour, he worked his way through a copy of the book, placing a small red dot next to each word and phrase that required fixing until—two long days and nights later—he had reached the last paragraph.

Then—before he could turn over the marked copy of the book to the publisher, and against his better judgment—Feifer lent the book to a friend who promised to guard it with his life. Instead, the friend mislaid the marked copy; he could not remember where, ex-

cept it was somewhere in London's vast Bayswater district. There was nothing Feifer could do but repeat the arduous task of adapting the book for an American audience.

The Girl from Petrovka enjoyed success on both sides of the Atlantic and received significant critical acclaim. Two years passed, and the story was about to be made into a movie with British actor Anthony Hopkins playing one of the leads. Two months before filming was to begin in Vienna, the diligent Hopkins sought to prepare for the role by reading the novel. But a trip to central London for a copy proved unfruitful—bookstores no longer stocked the book—and Hopkins headed home empty-handed.

But while waiting for a train in London's Leicester Square underground station, the actor noticed something lying on an otherwise empty bench. His first instinct was to back away; this was a time when terrorist bombs were exploding in London. Drawn by curiosity, however, Hopkins edged closer. It was a book. Gingerly picking it up, Hopkins was amazed to discover that it was *The Girl from Petrovka*.

Astonished and delighted, the actor took the volume, read it, and carried it with him to Vienna when filming began. There he met author Feifer, whom he immediately told of his amazing good fortune in finding a copy of the book. The author's polite interest turned to wide-eyed amazement as Hopkins finished his story. One thing distracted him as he read, said Hopkins: Hundreds of mysterious red dots speckled the pages.

Feifer realized immediately that Hopkins had found the very book that had been lost in Bayswater two years earlier. □

Finding Finn Again

Throughout his prosperous career as a lawyer in Buffalo, New York, in the late 1800s, James Fraser Gluck earned a reputation as a patron of learning. He was particularly generous to the lending library in Buffalo, then called the Young Men's Association, later the Buffalo and Erie County Public Library, on whose behalf, and with his own funds, he hunted down hundreds of notes, letters, autographs, and manuscripts by authors and celebrities. He obtained original works of authors Louisa May Alcott, Honoré de Balzac, and Henry Wadsworth Longfellow, British politician Benjamin Disraeli, American suffragist Susan B. Anthony—and former riverboat pilot and editor Samuel Langhorne Clemens, better known to the world as novelist and wit Mark Twain.

Gluck courted Twain, who had been a dues-paying member of the Young Men's Association when he lived in Buffalo for eighteen months from 1869 to 1871. During that time, Twain was editor of the *Buffalo Evening News*, which he co-owned with J. N. Larned, who later became superintendent of the Buffalo library. It was Gluck's practice simply to ask writers to send him manuscripts. Twain responded to a request for the manuscript of *Life on the Mississippi* in 1885 by sending instead the second half of *The Adventures of Huckleberry Finn*, along with an apology because the first half was lost, apparently mislaid by the printers.

Huckleberry Finn was published in London in 1884 and in the United States a few months later, re-

ceiving indifferent notices from critics. Early reviews notwithstanding, the book is now considered by many the greatest American novel ever written, a model for generations of later writers.

The first half of *Huckleberry Finn* disappeared from the sight of all but a handful of people for more than a century. Then, in 1990, the 600-page handwritten manuscript—covered with Twain's editorial changes—appeared again. It was found, not in Buffalo's library, but in one of six trunks once owned by James Gluck that were stored in the attic of one of his granddaughters, a librarian living in Hollywood, California.

The details of the manuscript's travels may never be known, but scholars have reconstructed the probable sequence of events as follows.

Although Twain could not find the first half of *Huckleberry Finn* and thought it lost, he apparently did forward it to Gluck two years later. Library superintendent Larned wrote to Twain in 1887 thanking him for the first half of the book.

For unknown reasons, the papers were in the home of James Gluck a decade later when Gluck died in New York City at the age of forty-five. Apparently they remained there until 1920, when the family moved to California. Among the family's belongings were six trunks. These remained in the possession of Gluck's daughter, Margaret, a violinist, until her death in 1961. They then were moved to the attic of the Hollywood home of Margaret Gluck's niece and James Gluck's granddaughter—a woman who, wishing to preserve her privacy, has asked that her name not be used.

And there the trunks rested until, one day in October 1990, the granddaughter was examining the contents of the trunks and came across a provocative package wrapped in brown paper and marked with the legend "Manuscript of Huckleberry Finn."

Ironically, the Buffalo museum's curator of rare books, William H.

Loos, just missed taking part in the discovery in 1983. At that time, he came across the granddaughter's name while looking for any correspondence Gluck may have had with the many authors whose works he collected. But Loos was unable to contact the woman or her sister—leaving the long-lost manuscript undisturbed for another seven years. When he learned of the discovery, Loos quipped, "We will consider it an overdue book and waive the fines." □

Author Mark Twain corrected the very first line of his manuscript *(below)* of *The Adventures of Huckleberry Finn*, the character depicted at left in an illustration from the original edition.

Read Herring

Prior to his days as a well-known novelist and playwright in nineteenth-century Germany, Hermann Sudermann made his living by submitting weekly installments of his novels to a newspaper in Berlin. One day the newspaper editor ordered an end to what he considered a precarious arrangement. Instead of delivering his novels chapter by chapter, in the future Sudermann was to complete the entire book. This would end the editor's worry that, if anything happened to the author, the readers would be left in suspense.

Sudermann, who had been paid as each chapter was published, was not pleased. The new practice would mean long periods without income. But he had no choice. So he sequestered himself on the family farm in East Prussia and started a new work entitled *Frau Sorge*, the story of a young man torn between devotion to his father and love for a woman. When the work was finished, Sudermann, eager for income after a long drought, set off to deliver it to the newspaper.

With the manuscript in his overcoat pocket, the author boarded a train for Berlin. At Insterburg, where he was to change trains, he met some old friends. Instead of

boarding the Berlin train immediately, he joined his comrades for an evening of revelry. Sudermann awoke the next morning in Berlin, but he had no memory of how he got there or what had happened the night before. Nervously, he groped for the manuscript in his overcoat pocket—and was horrified to discover that it was gone.

Dismayed at his own foolishness and what it had cost him, Sudermann started back to the farm and his writing table. That evening he again found himself waiting for a connecting train in Insterburg. Since the train was not due until morning, the author found lodgings, then began wandering from pub to pub, drowning his sorrows. Eventually, he stopped at a delicatessen and ordered a herring.

The fish was handed to him wrapped in the customary scrap paper, and Sudermann was already eating when he recognized the handwriting on it. The wrapping paper was, indeed, a page from his own manuscript. Overjoyed, the writer gathered the rest of the delicatessen's wrapping paper—and recovered nearly all of his novel.

Frau Sorge was published in 1887. It not only earned Sudermann a fee from the Berlin newspaper, but became recognized as his masterwork. □

The Bonanza in the Barn

For five years, antique dealer Jack Guerrera worked to gain the trust of a ninety-two-year-old woman who lived in the small town of Gansevoort, New York, not far from Guerrera's shop in the upstate town of Hudson Falls. Mrs. H., as the woman wished to be known to preserve her privacy, lived in a trailer, but the barn next to it held many old objects that Guerrera felt might be attractive to customers. At first, she was not interested in selling anything, but over the years she relented, allowing Guerrera to buy several aged and interesting items. Finally, in February of 1983, Mrs. H. agreed to allow the dealer to explore her barn.

The barn held the memorabilia of several generations of the family that occupied a house that once stood next to it. The house had burned down in the 1950s. Now books, trunks, furniture, and obsolete household items filled the barn's corners; parked among them was even a twenty-year-old car. The antique dealer had long since learned, however, that the greatest finds are often the least conspicuous. So his attention was drawn to an unobtrusive pile of boxes, covered with a stack of *Reader's Digest* magazines and plastic sheeting. He opened the top box and pulled out some papers: "First draught of *Typee*," he read. Searching further, he stumbled on several trunks marked with the name Melville.

That evening, Guerrera's wife explained the connection: *Typee*, she told him, was a South Seas romance written by nineteenth-

Melville family letters and a draft of Herman Melville's novel Typee rest by the family trunk in which they were discovered.

century novelist Herman Melville—the author, she reminded him, of the American classic *Moby Dick.*

Guerrera contacted John and Carolyn DeMarco, owners of The Lyrical Ballad Bookstore in nearby Saratoga Springs. The DeMarcos were avid antique-book collectors, and John DeMarco was a devoted student of Melville. He had recently given over two years to a chronological reading of all the author's works. Upon news of the discovery, DeMarco could barely contain himself. He knew that very little original Melville material was known to exist. Scholars believed the author had grown bit-

ter and discouraged late in his life and had burned his letters and manuscripts. If the writings Guerrera had found were Melville's, they would be invaluable to literary historians and critics. On the eve of his meeting with Guerrera, DeMarco spent the entire night searching his own collection for an example of Melville's handwriting that he could match against the papers from Mrs. H.'s barn.

The next morning in Gansevoort, DeMarco knew immediately that the papers were authentic. For two months, John and Carolyn DeMarco examined and organized the material; in addition to the draft of *Typee*, the trove included more than 500 Melville family letters. Providing rich details of Melville family life, these proved to be the

discovery's real prize. Scholars believe that Herman Melville's sister Augusta was responsible for saving the voluminous correspondence.

Mrs. H. and her husband inadvertently preserved them for posterity. Until 1930, the couple had lived in a historic home in Gansevoort once owned by the Melvilles, who were themselves descended from the family that gave the village its name. When the couple moved, some residual possessions of the Melvilles—including the long-forgotten and neglected letters of the author—went with them to be stored in the barn next to their new home. There, the author's legacy was preserved from the fire that later consumed Mrs. H.'s house, kept safe for Jack Guerrera's accidental discovery. □

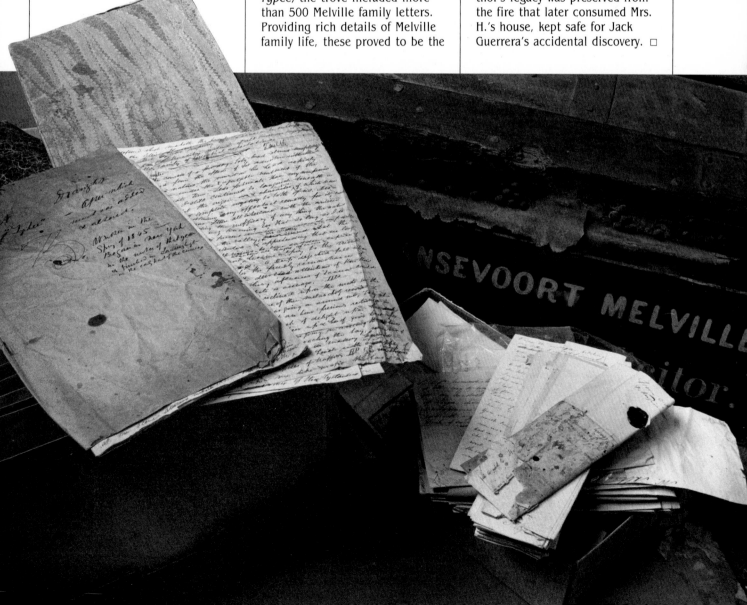

Fish Stories

In February of 1891, a lookout on the whaling ship *Star of the East*, sailing near the Falkland Islands, spotted a large sperm whale. Within minutes, two small boats were launched in pursuit. But as the craft neared its quarry, the whale smashed its tail on the water, creating turbulence that overturned one of the boats. Two crewmen were lost. Despite the tragedy, the whale was caught and killed. Its carcass was butchered—and the truth along with it. Certain *Star* shipmates swore that one of the lost harpooners, James Bartley, appeared inside the leviathan's cavernous stomach, unconscious but still alive. Bartley recuperated over the course of the next several weeks, the story went, remembering little of his ordeal except that the whale's belly had been deathly hot. But if the incident did not mark his memory, it left an indelible imprint on his appearance: Washed in the whale's stomach juices, Bartley's skin was bleached an unearthly white—the color it remained for the rest of his life.

The strange tale of this latter-day Jonah was told and retold for more than thirty years and was published in several magazines and books. Eventually it was revealed as a hoax, dreamed up by the crew of the whaling ship and swallowed by one and all.

Bartley's tale is one of hundreds, perhaps thousands, of sagas describing the loss and miraculous recovery of valued objects—or even people—from the bellies of various sea creatures. They are true fish stories, and most must be taken with a skepticism appropriate to the genre.

Consider the luck of James Price, who lost his dentures in Bull Shoals Lake, Arkansas. It was reported that, ten days after his misadventure, Price recovered his bridgework from the belly of a twenty-pound catfish. A similar tale is told of Ricky Shipman of Rock Hill, South Carolina, who lost his driver's license from the pocket of his bathing trunks. He had to wait eleven years before recovering it. Supposedly, a fisherman found the license in the stomach of a freshly caught mackerel.

Since before biblical times, creatures from seas, lakes, rivers, and castle moats have helped untold numbers of people—especially saints and other religious figures—when their beloved possessions plummeted into the murky depths. The item most frequently lost and found was a ring.

Kentigern, the patron saint of Glasgow, Scotland, was the protagonist of a sixth-century fish story. When the queen of Cadzow gave one of her rings to a nobleman, her jealous husband stole it from the favored knight and hurled it into the Clyde River. He then demanded that his wife find the ring or face death. Fortunately for the queen, Kentigern interceded. In no time, he had hooked a salmon and produced from its belly the missing ring. The grateful queen repented her sins and was saved. The event is memorialized in Glasgow's coat of arms, which depicts a salmon with a ring in its mouth.

Mrs. John Biddle of Mine Hill, New Jersey, was reportedly the beneficiary of a saintly pickerel on her first fishing trip. She hauled in an eleven-pounder—a fish big enough to become the subject of a believable fish story. But this pickerel, to her delight, carried in its stomach a lovely collection of jewels that had been stolen from the Biddles three years earlier. □

A Gem of an Illness

For several weeks during the summer of 1988, seventy-nine-year-old Virginia Argue of Roseville, California, complained of severe abdominal pains. In September, doctors pronounced their grim diagnosis: ovarian cancer.

The following month, surgeons operated, but no cancer was found. Instead, they removed a one-eighth-inch diamond, encased in a firm, fluid-filled cyst.

Argue and her doctors at Roseville Community Hospital speculated that the stone was accidentally left behind fifty-two years before, during the Cesarean delivery of her daughter, Sharon. □

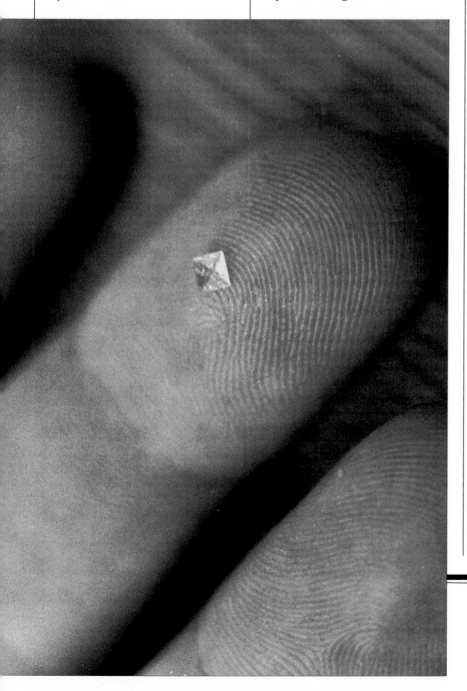

Double Discovery

William H. Jensen, a businessman in Browns Valley, Minnesota, was watching workers dump gravel one day in the fall of 1933 when one of them plucked something out of the growing pile. Thinking the fragment might be bone and knowing Jensen was an amateur archaeologist, the man asked whether Jensen could identify it. Indeed, it did appear to be bone.

Approaching the heap of gravel, Jensen began sifting through the stones, and before long, two similar fragments emerged. They appeared to be fossilized—their original bone replaced by minerals from the soil—and Jensen wondered if they could be human. He ordered an assistant to help examine the gravel, and within minutes they uncovered a perfect flint spearpoint—strong evidence that humans had indeed been somewhere around. Excited by the find, Jensen and his assistant sped to the local gravel pit.

There, Jensen examined a fresh wagonload of gravel. He immediately plucked out a stone knife, and his assistant found a spearpoint. Jensen eagerly scanned the gravel pit's wall and saw the pay dirt he sought—a patch of earth, stained brick red, located a few feet below the top of the gravel face. He could hardly contain his excitement: The red material was ocher, a mineral oxide often used by ancient peoples to line their burial pits.

Jensen's find was an intact human grave, and within it lay a skull, various other bones, several teeth, and a brown flint knife. ◊

The amateur archaeologist filled a five-gallon paint can with gravel from the base of the wall below the tomb and carried it home. Late into the night, he and his wife sifted through the stones, finding more bones, teeth, spearpoints, and other tools. Jensen was able to assemble the bones into a partial skeleton.

Browns Valley Man, as the skeleton came to be called, soon attracted the attention of Professor Albert Jenks, a prominent archaeologist with the University of Minnesota, who persuaded Jensen to loan him the bones for further study. In the mid-1930s, the professor published a number of articles about Browns Valley Man, alerting the scientific community to the skeleton's existence and suggesting a possible age of 8,000 to 12,000 years.

As promised, Jenks returned the skeleton when his examination was finished. For more than a decade, Jensen displayed Browns Valley Man to a steady stream of archaeologists, amateur and professional, eager to examine the find.

In 1950, Jensen, preparing to take his family on a trip, packed the skeleton away for safekeeping among his many other collected items. Other interests consumed his attention after the family's return, and the location of Browns Valley Man's latest resting place—like his first—slowly receded from memory.

When Jensen died in 1960, it appeared that the skeleton's whereabouts would never be known. Jensen's wife, who lived in the house until 1984, never found the bones. But in 1987, one of Jensen's sons-in-law found a box in a basement room. Inside, intact, was Browns Valley Man.

Within weeks, the remains again became the focus of intense study. New, more sophisticated processes revealed its age to be about 9,000 years. As Jensen and Jenks had perhaps hoped and suspected, Browns Valley Man—discovered twice since his death—is one of the best-preserved and most complete human skeletons of its period to be found in the Western Hemisphere. □

A farmer's wife in Germany lost her wedding ring in a field behind her house one day in the 1920s. Almost forty years later, the woman was delighted to find it—hidden in a potato that had been grown in that very field.

COINCIDENCE

Life without coincidence would be dull indeed. The chance meeting, the lifesaving encounter, the lost object that suddenly reappears—each is an example of life's sleight of hand, the seeming work of an unseen wizard who delights in his ability to astonish and confound. Some coincidences grow legends around them so that the events that they entail seem too good—or bad—to be true. Theories arise seeking to lend reason to such coincidences. Those individuals who have experienced the irrational force of happenstance, however, know that there is no reason. Good or bad, luck happens.

5

Jim-Jim

Jim Lewis and Jim Springer were identical twins separated shortly after their birth in Piqua, Ohio, and adopted by different families. But when they were finally reunited in 1979, nearly forty years after their separation, these two virtual strangers discovered that their lives had followed remarkably similar courses.

First, each lived about the same distance from his birthplace, Springer in Dayton and Lewis in Lima. Then there was the matter of names: Each named Jim by his adoptive parents, both grew up with adoptive brothers named Larry. The Jims married women named Linda and each had a son—one named James Alan, the other James Allan. Both Jims divorced and remarried women named Betty. And both of them had boyhood dogs named Toy.

At work and play, the twins were alike. Both had worked at McDonald's restaurants, at service stations, and then as deputy sheriffs. They might well have bumped into each other on vacation, since both favored the same stretch of beach in St. Petersburg, Florida.

Although Springer and Lewis were in reasonably good health when they met, each had survived a heart attack, endured the discomfort of hemorrhoids, and suf-

Pensively posed twins Jim Lewis (near right) and Jim Springer ponder their parallel lives.

Ties That Bind

Alfred Smith was driving home from his office in El Paso, Texas, one June evening in 1934 when he was halted by a dreadful accident. A motorcycle-mounted El Paso County highway patrolman had collided with a truck, demolishing the cycle and throwing patrolman Allen Falby into the street. When Smith arrived, Falby lay writhing in agony, his right leg nearly severed and blood gushing from a ruptured artery.

Recognizing Falby's as a life-or-death plight, Smith pulled off his necktie and tied a crude tourniquet around the policeman's leg to stanch the bleeding until an ambulance could arrive. Falby not only survived, but his leg was saved, and after several months' treatment, he returned to his job.

Almost five years after the accident, on December 12, 1938, Falby was patrolling on his motorcycle when he received a radio report of an accident. Reaching the scene before the ambulance, Falby found a car smashed into a tree, its driver pinned, unconscious, behind the steering wheel. His right pants leg was saturated with blood spurting from a severed artery. Falby quickly applied a tourniquet. Then, as he set about wresting the victim from the seat, the policeman found himself gazing dumbfounded into the face of Alfred Smith—the man who had tied a lifesaving tourniquet on Falby's own leg. □

fered tension headaches that turned into migraines. Both had had vasectomies. Both chewed their fingernails. For refreshment, both men drank Miller Lite beer. They chain-smoked Salem cigarettes. Neither enjoyed watching baseball; both preferred stock-car racing. Basement workshops allowed the Jims to pursue their interests in carpentry.

Domestically, they appeared to be as happily alike as bookends: Jim Springer and Jim Lewis enjoyed doing housework, partly because it gave them a chance to leave love notes to their wives scattered about the house.

And both men expressed joy at their reunion. □

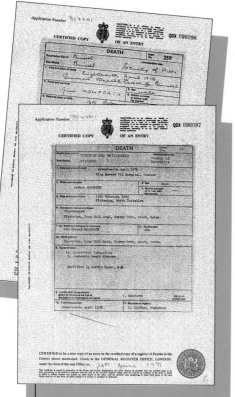

Twins to the End

Through sixty-six years of life, Jim and Arthur Mowforth had fulfilled their birthright as identical twins. Their interests were the same, their lives parallel. Both had made careers as air-squadron leaders in Britain's Royal Air Force.

And then they died as they had lived—identically. On the evening of April 17, 1975, Arthur was taken to a hospital in Windsor, west of London, experiencing severe chest pains. Within hours, Jim suffered the same symptoms and was rushed to a hospital in Bristol, eighty miles away. Both died of heart attacks soon after arriving at the hospitals. □

Names, by the Numbers

Not long after his hurried wartime wedding in 1940 Britain, soldier D. J. Page (in military uniform at right) rushed off to rejoin his army unit. Soon he received his wedding pictures in the mail—only to discover that they had already been opened by someone else. Soon he discovered that the culprit was as much a dupe of coincidence as Page himself.

Page's military unit was Troop B. One of the soldiers in the adjoining Troop A was named Pape. Pape's military identification number was 1509322, different from Page's (1509321) only by a single digit. Their mail mix-up continued until Page was finally reassigned.

After the war, Pape and Page crossed paths once more, again with troublesome consequences. Page, a driver with London Transport, noticed one day that his paycheck was smaller than usual. It turned out that his records had been confused with those of another driver, who had just been transferred to the garage in southwest London. The reason for the confusion was immediately apparent: The other driver was Pape, and his license number was 29223. Page's was 29222. □

Wanda Wonder

Wanda Marie Johnson of Adelphi, Maryland, had no intention of leading a double life. But for three years in the late 1970s, her identity became mysteriously intertwined with that of an alter ego.

The first inkling that something was wrong occurred when Johnson visited her doctor at Howard University Hospital in 1975. She found that her medical records were scrambled; together with her name and social security number was someone else's medical history.

Other problems soon popped up. When Johnson's daughter was born, the hospital sent a bill for delivery of a boy. Credit collectors began calling about unpaid bills for things she had never bought. When she applied for a Maryland driver's permit, state officials told her she already had a license. She had to convince them otherwise.

When Johnson bought a new Ford Granada in 1977, the car's registration provided the first clue to the puzzle. The envelope containing the registration was addressed to Wanda Marie Johnson in Suitland, Maryland, twelve miles away. The Postal Service had misdirected it to Adelphi. Sure enough, the telephone directory showed what Johnson by now suspected: Another Wanda Marie Johnson lived in Suitland.

Conversation between the Wanda Marie Johnsons revealed still more coincidental similarities. Both were born on June 15, 1953, and lived in the District of Columbia before moving to nearby Prince George's County in Maryland. Both still worked in the District. Both were mothers of two children born at Howard University Hospital. Both were the eldest of three children, each having a sister and a brother. The husband of the Suitland Johnson once worked with the Adelphi Johnson.

As if calculated to lead creditors and bureaucrats astray, the first four digits of their social security numbers were identical. At the time they became acquainted, both women owned 1977 two-door Ford Granadas whose eleven-digit serial numbers differed only in their last three digits.

The story of the two Wanda Marie Johnsons is indeed true, if exceedingly unlikely: One expert estimates that the odds against such a train of coincidences are one trillion to one. □

Wanda Marie Johnson of Adelphi, Maryland, _(near right)_ meets Wanda Marie Johnson of Suitland, Maryland.

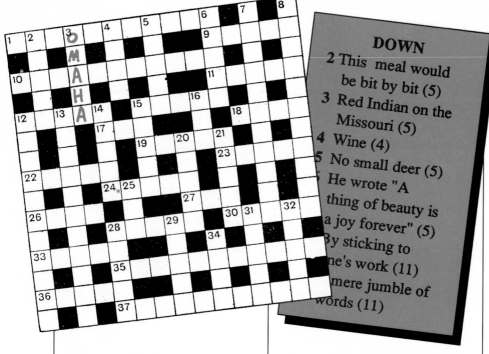

DOWN

2 This meal would be bit by bit (5)

3 Red Indian on the Missouri (5)

4 Wine (4)

5 No small deer (5)

He wrote "A thing of beauty is a joy forever" (5)

By sticking to ne's work (11)

mere jumble of words (11)

Innocent crossword clues led to a troubling solution in London's *Daily Telegraph* days before D-Day—the code name OMAHA for the principal beach to be assaulted.

Puzzling Tactics

A few days before D-Day—the Allied armies' invasion of Nazi-occupied Europe on June 6, 1944—British counterintelligence agents swarmed into the Fleet Street offices of the *London Daily Telegraph*. They expected to arrest the erudite geniuses responsible for one of the cleverest espionage schemes of World War II.

For the month preceding the massive invasion, code words used in the top-secret D-Day preparations repeatedly appeared as answers to the *Telegraph's* popular daily crossword puzzles. On May 3, the solution to a four-letter word for "one of the United States" was *Utah*. Military planners cringed, for this was the code name for one of two French beaches where American forces planned to land. The other beach was coded Omaha, and that name turned up as the answer to a clue in the May 22 puzzle, "red Indian on the Missouri."

Eight days later—now less than a week before the invasion—the puzzle asked for the name of a bush that is "a centre of nursery revolutions." The answer: *Mulberry*, around which children dance a nursery rhyme. It also happened to be the code name for the concrete harbor facilities the Allies planned.

On June 2, nearly on the eve of the hush-hush operation, the *Telegraph* printed two puzzle solutions, each containing a word that fairly leaped off the page—a page that by now was carefully scrutinized every day by concerned investigators: The solutions to the previous Saturday's puzzle included the word *Overlord*, the blanket code name for the entire D-Day invasion; and the solution to the June 1 puzzle included *Neptune*, the code for Overlord's naval operations. That was the final straw. Counterintelligence agents descended on the newspaper.

When they arrived, the agents discovered a foggy schoolmaster, Leonard Sidney Dawe, the senior crossword compiler who had been devising the newspaper's puzzles for more than twenty years. Dawe was interrogated, but the agents concluded that he was no nefarious Nazi spy, even though he could offer no reason why the code words sprang from his mind at that sensitive time. The agents remained as puzzled as the puzzle master.

If the puzzle was part of a spy plot, it was singularly unsuccessful. Operation Overlord caught German forces by surprise. □

Aid from an Aussie

During World War I, E. G. Steele, a hotheaded British gunner stationed in France, was court-martialed and convicted of striking an officer. As punishment, he was tied to a gun wheel for an hour at sundown each day for ten days.

But a passing group of Australian soldiers thought the discipline was harsh and degrading. One of their officers persuaded the British commander to end the sentence, and an Australian soldier cut Steele loose. The gunner noticed that his benefactor was missing two fingers from his left hand.

Ten years later, E. G. Steele was riding the subway in New York City when he detected the unmistakable Australian accent of the man sitting next to him. Steele began to tell his fellow rider about the good deed that an Australian had done for him in France. But the Australian rider interrupted and finished Steele's story himself. Then he raised his left hand. It was missing two fingers. □

Plum Strange

Few foods are more closely identified with England than plum pudding, a dense, brandy-soaked, steamed confection as much a part of a British Christmas as song and gifts. Perhaps because of its British origin, the dessert has been almost universally shunned by the French, who often judge their own cuisine superior to all others. But at least one French native—the distinguished nineteenth-century French poet Emile Deschamps—developed a lifelong passion for plum pudding, a fondness that led to two improbable reunions.

Deschamps was introduced to the dessert as a youngster attending a boarding school in Orléans. There, one of the schoolmasters, a Monsieur de Fortgibu, had just returned from England and was eager to share a slice of his discovery. The young Deschamps found the pudding rich, sweet, and, to a degree, intoxicating. The encounter was memorable but not to be repeated very often.

Ten years later, the poet peered into the window of a restaurant on the Boulevard Poissoniere in Paris. There, against all odds, he spied a plum pudding. But when he went into the restaurant and requested a piece—the pudding is usually shared—he was told that it was reserved for another customer. Deschamps, crestfallen, turned to leave. Before he reached the street, however, he heard the restaurateur call to his customer, "Monsieur de Fortgibu! Would you have the goodness to share your plum pudding with this gentleman?" The other diner was indeed the schoolmaster who had introduced Deschamps to plum pudding.

More years passed. Fortgibu and plum pudding had become footnotes to Deschamps's busy life, until, one evening, the poet attended a dinner party where his hosts proudly served English plum pudding. Deschamps consumed the dessert with delight and entertained the other guests with his tale of plum pudding and coincidence. The only thing lacking that evening, he concluded with a smile, was Fortgibu.

No sooner had Deschamps spoken than there came a knock on the door, and an aged Monsieur de Fortgibu hobbled into the room. Both he and Deschamps were nonplussed. The poet was certain that his hosts had staged the reunion as a prank. Fortgibu, however, knew otherwise. He, too, had received an invitation to dinner that evening—with other hosts, in another apartment. He had simply knocked at the wrong door. □

An eagerly awaited, steaming plum pudding is presented at the end of an English family's Christmas dinner.

Bach and Forth

Long before he won fame for writing the whimsical best-selling adventure *Jonathan Livingston Seagull*, Richard Bach was a passionate flier and collector of rare old planes. Bach was also an occasional barnstormer, hopping from place to place in his unusual airborne antiques, giving rides and performing stunts.

In 1966, Bach's barnstorming vehicle was a Detroit-Parks Speedster, a wood and wire biplane covered with colorful fabric. The plane, one of only eight in existence, was built in 1929. Parts were difficult to come by, and Bach guarded his prize jealously. Nevertheless, one day in Palmyra, Wisconsin, he allowed a friend to fly his prized craft. Predictably, the friend crashed on landing.

Although the pilot was unhurt, the plane was grievously injured: One wheel was gone, the right shock absorber was broken, and both wings were badly damaged. Nevertheless, Bach and his friend managed to repair the entire craft—all but one wing strut. Bach assumed, given the rarity of the plane, that a replacement strut would never be found and that he would have to fabricate a new one.

As his despair deepened, Bach was accosted by an old pilot named Stan Gerlach. Gesturing around the field and to three near-by hangers that he owned, Gerlach announced that the buildings—and the field itself—were littered with old airplane junk, some of it dating back as far as 1924. He never sold airplane parts to make a profit, the old pilot said, but those who needed them could help themselves. Bach thanked Gerlach, but repeated his pessimistic assessment of the situation: They would never find a strut for a Detroit-Parks.

Gerlach, smiling, pointed to a heap of parts—the remains of a neglected airplane—lying no more than ten feet from where they stood. In the pile was the strut that Bach needed. □

Standing before his antique Detroit-Parks Speedster, author-barnstormer Richard Bach swaps tales with aircraft builder Oliver Parks (left) and Leon Seltzer of Parks College of St. Louis University (right).

Sherman's March

To C. E. Sherman (below), the respected chairman of the civil-engineering department at Ohio State University in Columbus, the conclusion of the task before him seemed to recede even as he worked. He was charged with compiling the 1909 Ohio State Highway Atlas. For months he gathered the maps needed from cities, towns, and counties throughout Ohio. The data accumulated, but a yawning gap existed in information about Pike and Highland counties in southern Ohio, where the U.S. Geological Survey had not yet drawn maps. Sherman's best resources—if he could find them—were old county maps and atlases. Lacking them, the state atlas could be completed only after an arduous and expensive survey, for which Sherman had neither time nor money.

Letters had produced no information, so Sherman decided that he had no option but to visit the two counties and search records himself. He set out early one Saturday morning in August, expecting to be on the road at least a week, maybe two. The first stop was the U.S. Army Corps of Engineers office in Cincinnati, where he picked up the last available copy of an Ohio River map that was renowned for its accuracy. The map, which had eluded Sherman for months, was a requirement for checking other information. It cost eighty-five cents.

Onward Sherman traveled that Saturday, first toward Highland County. Waiting for a train in Norwood, midway in the journey from Cincinnati, the engineer struck up a conversation with the ticket agent. When the engineer told of his quest for old maps and atlases, the agent responded, "There's an old book like that in the rear room." Indeed there was: Under the dusty stacks they discovered an old Highland County atlas.

The second of his three goals met, Sherman changed his itinerary and struck out by train for Pike County. As he stepped from the train that afternoon in the county seat of Waverly, the professor bumped into one of his only two acquaintances there. The man walked Sherman to his hotel and promised to send Sherman's other friend if he could be found. The second friend showed up after dinner. No, he did not know of any Pike County maps, but his father might. As if on cue, the father appeared at the hotel. He knew of no maps, but the county auditor might.

By now the uncommon had become ordinary: The auditor strode through the lobby door. Although it was Saturday night, this authority cheerfully led Sherman across the street to the courthouse and unlocked his office. There on the wall was an excellent old map of Pike County, which the professor copied. For no apparent reason, he had stuffed a piece of tracing paper into his bag that morning—and the paper was precisely the size of the wall map.

Sherman slept well that evening, having completed his task in about twelve hours of successive coincidences. □

Smash Hit

Following a full season on Broadway in 1928, the American company of Noël Coward's revue *This Year of Grace* toured briefly through Canada. It was there, during a matinee performance in London, Ontario, that a gaffe by the revue's star, the British comedienne Beatrice Lillie *(left)*, turned into a lifesaving act.

Phyllis Harding was a member of the show's chorus, which was lined up across one side of the stage near the close of one scene. Just after Lillie completed the second verse of the scene's musical finale, *Britannia Rules the Waves,* the chorus was to move to center stage. The fortunate Harding later described what actually happened: "I suddenly caught in her [Lillie's] eye a look of anguish, and to our amazement we suddenly realized that she was repeating the entire second verse all over again—keeping us glued to our places on the stage, unable to move." The orchestra caught up with the singer and covered the blunder. The song continued.

"Suddenly," Harding said, "there was a resounding crash, and one of the biggest arc lights fell in the middle of the empty stage—where by rights at that moment we should have been standing. Without a flicker, Miss Lillie calmly went on to the chorus, and obediently we moved into our positions covering the entire stage." □

Bride's Bane

When the princess Maria del Pozzo della Cisterna wed the duke of D'Aosta, son of the king of Italy, on May 30, 1867, the festivities were marred by such a tragic tangle of events that the royal family suppressed the truth, lest the very news bring misfortune to the couple's life.

The ominous events began before the wedding, when the bride's wardrobe mistress hanged herself, prompting the superstitious princess to order a new gown. The ceremony itself was delayed twice. First, the mounted officer appointed to lead the wedding procession from the palace to the church suffered sunstroke and collapsed. Then the palace gates failed to open for the matrimonial procession. The gatekeeper was found nearby, lying in a pool of blood.

Fate tendered a reprieve during the ceremony, but minutes after, the best man—probably ineptly handling his ceremonial weapon—shot himself in the head. Eventually, the bride and groom were escorted by a procession of carriages to the railway station, where the royal newlyweds were to board a train for their honeymoon. More trouble dogged their steps: The official who had drawn up the marriage contract suffered a stroke, and the anxious stationmaster fell under the wheels of the approaching bridal locomotive.

King Victor Emmanuel, by now dishonored by the series of misfortunes and convinced that the ceremony, and everything associated with it, was jinxed, refused to allow anyone aboard the train and tried desperately to return the procession to the safety of the palace.

But it was not to be. Riding alongside the bridal carriage, the count of Castiglione fell from his horse underneath the carriage's wheels. The count died when the weight of the wheels drove a splendid medal through his uniform into his chest. □

AMEDEO DI SAVOIA, Duca d'Aosta, sposato il 30 Maggio 1867.

MARIA DAL POZZO, Principessa della Cisterna, sposata il 30 Maggio 1867.

Holes in One

During the Massachusetts tax uprising known as Shays's Rebellion, troops held off a group of insurgents who attacked the federal arsenal in Springfield on January 25, 1787. Among the attackers killed that day was Jabez Spicer of Leyden, Massachusetts. At the time, Spicer was wearing a coat that his brother Daniel had worn three years earlier when he was shot in a gun battle with Vermont militiamen. After Jabez's death only one bullet hole could be found in the coat. The shot that killed Jabez had passed precisely through the hole made by the shot that killed Daniel. □

A nineteenth-century engraving depicts rebels led by Daniel Shays *(foreground)* attacking the federal arsenal at Springfield, Massachusetts, in January of 1787.

Prussian Roulette

The placid springtime beauty of Berlin's famous boulevard Unter den Linden was shattered in May of 1866 when a student named Ferdinand Cohen-Blind fired four pistol shots at point-blank range at the Prussian premier, Prince Otto von Bismarck. Somehow, two bullets missed entirely. Two others wounded the Iron Chancellor, but true to his nickname, Bismarck appeared one week later, mounted and apparently healthy despite injury to his shoulder and lung. Cohen-Blind was arrested. His revolver was given to Bismarck—a souvenir of a near tragedy whose echo would ring out twice more.

In 1886, at Friedrichsruh, the Bismarck country home near Hamburg, the family was entertaining guests one evening. As the men retired to smoke cigars and talk politics, the ladies toured the castle. The assassin's pistol lay in its case on a writing table in the study. Princess Bismarck pointed it out and told of the attack and her husband's fortunate survival. It is not clear who handled the weapon, but suddenly the Princess's narrative was interrupted by a brilliant flash and roar. A fifth cartridge in the revolver's cylinder had fired. When the chancellor and his friends dashed in, they found the smoking gun on the floor, the acrid odor of gunpowder in the air, and the princess and her guests startled and upset, if uninjured. Bismarck angrily ordered that no one ever handle the gun again.

The dictate was obeyed for twenty years, until one rainy day in 1906. On that unfortunate day, the visiting son of a Bismarck cousin who had witnessed the accidental discharge in 1886 was guiding several guests around Friedrichsruh. When they reached the study, the young man told the tale of the fifth bullet. He neared the climax: "Some ladies were visiting the house," he said, "and one of them took up the pistol and foolishly pulled the trigger—like this"—

and he raised the legendary pistol.

Once more, light, sound, and the harsh smell of gunpowder filled the air. This time, as it had forty years before, blood flowed from a Bismarck's body. The sixth and last bullet loaded by Cohen-Blind four decades before tore into the young cousin's bicep. □

In an attack documented by a contemporary engraver, stunned onlookers recoil as Ferdinand Cohen-Blind fires on Prince Otto von Bismarck.

He Lost His Head

Louis XVI, king of France during the late eighteenth century and husband of Marie Antoinette, was warned as a child by an astrologer that the twenty-first day of the month was an unlucky one for him. Throughout his life, the ever-fearful Louis made it a point to avoid all business on that day. His precautions, however, were to no avail, and the date did prove unfortunate in every way.

On June 21, 1770, four years before he became king, Louis squired Marie into Paris, where their arrival in the Place de la Concorde was celebrated by a large crowd with music and fireworks. The joy was short-lived, however. A rocket misfired, roared into the merrymakers, and touched off a panic in which some 1,200 people were trampled to death and another 2,000 injured.

Louis lost again on June 21, 1791, when he and his queen were arrested at Varennes as they tried to flee the bloody French Revolution. A year later, on September 21, France abolished the monarchy. Finally, on January 21, 1793, Louis's life was cut short by the blade of a guillotine. □

France's King Louis XVI and Marie Antoinette are arrested by revolutionaries on June 21, 1791 *(upper engraving)*, and Louis is led to the guillotine on January 21, 1793 *(lower painting)*.

Matched Up

Thirty years before he became England's King Edward VII in 1901, the Prince of Wales presented a gold matchbox shaped like a portmanteau to actor Edward A. Sothern. The gift was a memento of their many fox-hunting adventures together. Soon after receiving the prince's present, however, Sothern lost it when he was thrown by his mount during a hunt. The fields were searched and a reward was posted to no avail, so Sothern had a duplicate made by the goldsmith who had fashioned the original.

Some years later, the actor gave the replica box to his eldest son, Sam, as Sam embarked on a business trip to Australia. The son, in turn, gave the duplicate box to a Mr. Labertouche as a token of gratitude for his help during Sam's visit down under. It now seemed that neither matchbox, despite its sentimental place in the Sothern family, would ever be seen again.

In fact, chance dictated otherwise.

Like his father, Sam Sothern was a passionate fox hunter. One day nearly twenty years after his father was given the original box—the elder Sothern had by now died—Sam was out with the hounds in the company of an elderly farmer, who had good news and a gift for the astonished son: That very morning one of the farmer's hands had found Edward A. Sothern's original matchbox.

Excited by the discovery, Sam described the incident in a letter to his brother, Edward H. Sothern, who was an actor then touring in America. Amused by the coincidence, Edward related the extraordinary tale to an Australian actor named Arthur Lawrence who had just joined Sothern's theater company. "I wonder what became of the duplicate?" Edward mused.

The answer was swift and surprising: Tugging on his watch chain, Lawrence displayed the charm—a gift, he said, from Sam Sothern's Australian friend Labertouche. □

An enthusiastic fox hunter, the Prince of Wales—later, King Edward VII—is depicted riding to hounds in a contemporary illustration.

A 1680 Dutch engraving depicts the
devastation wrought by the fire that
raged through Tokyo in 1657.

Killer Kimono

In February of 1657, a priest in Tokyo undertook to destroy a kimono whose unlucky aura was blamed for the illnesses and deaths of three teenage girls who had owned it. But instead of exorcising the demon, he appeared to release it to awful new heights of destructiveness.

As the fathers of the three young victims stood witness, the priest applied a torch to the kimono. The cloth burst into flames and the fire rose. Then, a turbulent wind blew in, and the kimono's reputed evil spirit seemed to assume control of events. The roaring flames quickly spread through Tokyo's traditional wood and paper buildings. When the inferno subsided, 100,000 people were dead, and three-fourths of the city was in ashes. □

Mummy Dearest

King Tutankhamen, Egyptian pharaoh of the fourteenth century BC, died young—he was only eighteen years old. His reputation lived on, however, thanks in part to a curse said to apply to those who disturbed his tomb. Although little credence is now given to the curse, striking coincidences have been associated with the tomb.

Tutankhamen's solid gold coffin, gold portrait mask, and other treasures remained undisturbed for more than 3,000 years until archaeologist Howard Carter, financed by Britain's Lord Carnarvon, uncovered the tomb on November 4, 1922, in Thebes, once the ancient capital of Egypt. Car-

ter's search had consumed years and had gathered a mythic reputation of its own. Little wonder, then, that superstitious Egyptian workers gave credit for the find not to the hardworking Carter, but to a canary—"the golden bird," they called it. Carter had bought the bird just days before finding the tomb, and the laborers connected the two events, concluding that the canary had brought good luck.

Soon after the discovery, an eerily humanlike cry pierced the air around Carter's house in Egypt; it was the dying voice of the canary as a cobra slunk into its cage and swallowed it. Villagers believed the serpent had come alive and slith-

ered from the pharaoh's headdress, where its image symbolized power, and struck the canary for betraying the secret of the tomb.

Soon the legend of the curse was revived and confabulated. In London, Cairo, and New York, speculation spread, even finding space in such sober newspapers as the *New York Times*. On March 19, 1923, Lord Carnarvon entered a Cairo hospital for treatment of an infected mosquito bite. Eighteen days later, at age fifty-three, he died of pneumonia. Reports soon spread—virtually unconfirmable years later—that at the moment of his death, the lights blinked out throughout Cairo; in England, Car-

Lincoln Saved

On Good Friday, April 14, 1865, actor John Wilkes Booth burst into the box in Ford's Theater occupied by President Abraham Lincoln, his wife, and their guests and assassinated the president. Scarcely a year before, another Lincoln was nearly killed on a railroad platform in Jersey City, New Jersey.

At that time, an impatient crowd shoved the president's oldest son, Robert Todd Lincoln, toward the path of a departing train. Tragedy was averted when an alert bystander dropped his baggage and, with ticket clenched in his teeth, hauled the young Lincoln back to safety by the collar of his overcoat.

According to a later account by Robert Lincoln, when he turned to thank his rescuer, he recognized a face "well known to me." Indeed it was. Before him stood Edwin Booth, one of the period's most famous actors—and the brother of John Wilkes Booth. □

Lord Carnarvon and Howard Carter (above, from right) pose with unidentified visitors near the mouth of King Tutankhamen's ancient tomb.

narvon's dog howled and died.

The dreaded curse appeared to be suspended for years afterward. But in 1966, another curious tragedy revived it. French officials wanted to exhibit Tutankhamen artifacts in Paris. Mohammed Ibrahim, director of the Cairo museum's department of antiquities, objected at first, then relented under political pressure. Immediately after Ibrahim gave his consent, his daughter was injured in an automobile accident. Ibrahim supposedly then dreamed that he would suffer a similar fate unless he stopped the exhibit. He failed to dissuade the French, and two days after his futile effort, Ibrahim was hit by a car and killed. □

Robert Todd Lincoln, then a student at Harvard College, was photographed in 1862, two years before his narrow escape from death.

Family Ties

Author Joseph Bryan III *(below)*, scion of an old Virginia family, wrote about his kin in a book on the Civil War, *The Sword over the Mantel.* Bryan concludes the book with an inscription that appears on a bronze tablet memorializing a minor Civil War skirmish that took place at his grandfather's home near Richmond.

"At this point," reads the inscription, "Confederate forces on March 1, 1864, repulsed Kilpatrick's raid."

This was the last passage Bryan typed as he finished the book in 1960. At the time, he was living on the Mediterranean island of Majorca. He bundled up his manuscript, delivered it to the post office, and hurried off to lunch at the home of friends. The rest of the guests were strangers to him, so Bryan was duly introduced at the table. His hostess noted that he hailed from Richmond.

The man across the table, also an American, responded immediately. "Richmond? I've often wanted to go there," he said, "but at the last minute something always prevented it." Smiling, he added, "Come to think of it, my grandfather had the same experience."

Surprising himself as much as anybody—but with the final words of the book still fresh in his memory—Bryan asked, "Is your name Kilpatrick, sir?" No, replied the stranger, but that was the name of his grandfather—the Union officer who had been repulsed on Bryan's own family lands almost 100 years before. □

Food for Thought

In his 1838 mystery tale, *The Narrative of Arthur Gordon Pym of Nantucket,* Edgar Allan Poe *(above)* told a macabre story of shipwrecked seamen adrift many days in an open lifeboat. Starving and nearly delirious, they drew straws to determine which one should die "to preserve the existence of the others." The sailor who proposed the cannibalism lost the draw and was killed and eaten. His name was Richard Parker.

Nearly a half-century later, three survivors of a shipwrecked English merchant vessel, *Mignonette,* were executed for the murder of a fourth crew member under similar circumstances. The real-life victim's name: Richard Parker. □

Icy Echoes

Fourteen years before the luxury liner *Titanic* sank on her maiden voyage, the tragedy was recounted in detail by an American novelist. So striking were the similarities between his fictional version and the real event that some people suspected paranormal forces at work. Given the well-known hazards of North Atlantic voyages, however, most observers chalk up the re-semblances to inevitable—if uncanny—coincidence.

The real-life *Titanic,* ballyhooed as "unsinkable" by the White Star Line, was carrying 2,227 passengers and crew from England to New York when it struck an iceberg late at night on April 14, 1912. By the early hours of April 15, the ship had sunk with a loss of more than 1,500 lives—among them some of the most prominent men and women of the decade.

The *Titanic* tragedy came eerily close to life imitating art. In 1898, American author Morgan Robertson published *Futility,* a short novel in which a giant luxury liner, the *Titan,* undertook a tragic maiden voyage across the Atlantic—also in April. The *Titan's* description nearly matched that of the later *Titanic:* Both were driven by three propellers and steamed at high speed, the *Titan* at twenty-five knots, the *Titanic* at twenty-three. They were more than 800 feet long, and both ships bore the wealthy glitterati of two continents. Like the *Titanic,* the *Titan* was deemed unsinkable and its lifeboats were considered a superfluous legal requirement. In both cases, the inadequate supply of lifeboats contributed to the casualty count. Like the *Titanic,* the fictional *Titan* collided with an iceberg, sustained a hole in its starboard side, and sank with great loss of life. Both events took place in the same area of the ocean.

If Robertson's novel was a coincidental herald of the *Titanic* tragedy, a later incident furnished a faint echo. Twenty-three years after the *Titanic* sank, on an inky April night in 1935, British seaman William C. Reeves stood watch on a coal ship steaming in the vicinity of the earlier sinking. When an iceberg suddenly loomed before Reeves, he quickly took action, and the ship narrowly averted a collision. Soon, however, Reeves's ship ran afoul of a field of icy debris that disabled her propeller, and she had to be towed to a repair yard at St. John's, Newfoundland.

The name of William Reeves's vessel was the *Titanian.* The sailor was born on the night of April 14, 1912—as the great *Titanic* slid to her watery grave. □

A contemporary newspaper illustration re-creates the "unsinkable" *Titanic*'s catastrophic collision with an iceberg in the North Atlantic.

Blowing in the Wind

An avid collector of stories concerning coincidences, the notable nineteenth-century French scientist Camille Flammarion claimed several firsthand encounters with chance. One occurred in Paris on a summer's day as Flammarion was finishing his book *L'Atmosphere,*

Encounter in Paris

Occasionally, real life takes on a storybook quality, as novelist Anne Parrish *(above)* discovered on her first visit to Paris in the 1920s. One warm June evening, while she and her husband were browsing in a bookstall along the river Seine, Parrish spied a dingy copy of an English children's book, *Jack Frost and Other Stories.* The old volume brought back a flood of fond memories of her childhood in Colorado Springs, Colorado, where she had last seen a copy of the book.

Parrish excitedly passed the book on to her husband. Much less impressed with the discovery than she, he dutifully opened the dog-eared book. Then, suddenly transfixed, he silently handed the volume back, pointing to something that his wife evidently had missed. There on the flyleaf, in the unskilled scrawl of a small child, were written the name and the address of the book's one-time owner: "Anne Parrish, 209 N. Weber Street, Colorado Springs." □

which was published in 1871.

Suddenly, a powerful gust blew open a window in his study and swept up a number of pages of his chapter. The purloined sheets fluttered to the pavement outside, where they scattered under the chestnut trees along Avenue de l'Observatoire. The wind was immediately followed by a downpour. Assuming the pages of his work to be irretrievable, Flammarion nev-er even bothered pursuing them.

Nevertheless, proof sheets of the windblown chapter arrived a few days later from Lahure's, Flammarion's printing house a few blocks away. Just one page was missing. When the astonished author inquired, he discovered that a porter for the printer had happened along on the stormy afternoon and retrieved the scattered papers. The porter, who had delivered part of Flammarion's manuscript earlier that day, assumed he had dropped the pages on his previous delivery; he carefully rearranged them and took them to the typesetter.

The subject of Flammarion's windswept, rescued chapter: the force of the wind. □

His desk piled high with manuscripts and papers, Camille Flammarion works next to an open window in his book-lined study.

ACKNOWLEDGMENTS

The editors wish to thank these individuals and institutions for their valuable assistance:

Irene Adams, Yale University Library, New Haven, Connecticut; Susan Albrecht, Binion's Horseshoe Hotel, Las Vegas; Scott Anfinson, Fort Smelling History Center, St. Paul, Minnesota; Daniel Aubry, Société des Bains de Mer, Monte Carlo; Red Barber, Tallahassee, Florida; David Barton, Kansas City Police Department, Kansas City, Missouri; Sharon Bidwell, *The Courier Journal*, Louisville, Kentucky; Linda Blye, Old Saybrook, Connecticut; Stuart Bostrom, Roseville, California; Bridgeport Public Library, Bridgeport, Connecticut; Guido Buldrini, ANSA, Rome; John Burch, Warren, Arkansas; Barbara Cairney, Shakespeare Guild Inc., Stratford, Connecticut; Maria-Fede Caproni, Rome; Cliff Charpentier, Fantasy Sports Inc., St. Paul, Minnesota; Donald Cloudsley, Buffalo and Erie County Public Library, Buffalo, New York; Giuseppe Colombo, Biblioteca Civica, Monza; Giancarlo Costa, Milan; Vernell Crittendon, Warden's Office, San Quentin, California; Paul Daniluk, Denver; Tanya Daniluk, Denver; Delaware State Lottery, Dover; Ray De Leon, Twin Cities Police Department, Larkspur, California; John DeMarco, Saratoga Springs, New York; Giorgio Dolci, Monopoli di Stato, Rome; Jana Drvota, Ohio State University Media Center, University Archives, Columbus, Ohio; Paul Dworin, Gaming & Wagering Business, New York; Robert Eberwein, Deutsche Bundesbank, Frankfurt; George Feifer, Sharon,

Connecticut; Nanette Fok, Asian Art Museum, San Francisco; Carey Garner, The Austin Historical Center, Austin, Texas; Ira Gitlin, Riverdale, Maryland; Casey Greene, Rosenberg Library, Galveston, Texas; Henry Grossi, Washington, D.C.; Ara Güler, Istanbul; James Hahn, Cape Girardeau, Missouri; Tracy Hanlon, South Carolina Department of Corrections, Columbia; Don Hinton, Twin Cities Police Department, Larkspur, California; Hoosier Lottery, Indianapolis; Illinois Lottery, Springfield; Susan Jarvis, University of Nevada Gaming Center, Las Vegas; Edward Kamuda, Titanic Historical Society, Indian Orchard, Massachusetts; Roberta House Kelly, La Center, Kentucky; John Kilbracken, House of Lords, London; Hieronymus Koestler, Verband Deutscher Geigenbauer, Stuttgart; Arne Laing, Stardust Sports Service, Las Vegas; Arthur Larsen, San Leandro, California; Jacqueline Lebailly, Chef de Gamme des Produits Loterie, France-Loto, Neuilly sur Seine; Philippe Le Leyzour, Musée des Granges de Port-Royal, Magny-les-Hameaux, France; Tom Leonard, Department of Statistics, University of Wisconsin, Madison; Jim Lewis, Elida, Ohio; Sheri Long, Palace Station Hotel and Casino, Las Vegas; Ronald McCoy, Emporia State University, Social Science Division, Emporia, Kansas; Ted Manno, Delaware Lottery Commission, Dover; Maryland State Lottery, Baltimore; Roy Melton, East Flat Rock, North Carolina; Johnny Moss, Binion's Horseshoe Hotel, Las Vegas; Frank Mowery, Folger Shakespeare Library, Washington, D.C.;

Laura Mulloy, Kansas City Police Department, Kansas City, Missouri; Alexandra Murphy, Williamstown, Missouri; New York State Division of the Lottery, Albany; John P. Nolan, American University, Washington, D.C.; Jack Paster, Swampscott, Massachusetts; John Allen Paulos, Temple University, Philadelphia; Pennsylvania Lottery, Middletown; Janet Jensen Presley, Edina, Minnesota; Franca Principe, Istituto e Museo di Storia della Scienza, Florence; Sonny Reizner, Rio Hotel and Casino, Las Vegas; Howard Robertson, Amtrak, Washington, D.C.; Gloria Rosenthal, Valley Stream, New York; Sarah Rossbach, New York; Lupe Salinas, 351st District Court, Houston; Sylvia Schoske, Staatliche Sammlung Agyptischer Kunst, Munich; Orrin Shane, Science Museum of Minnesota, St. Paul; Clarence Shangraw, Asian Art Museum, San Francisco; Theresa Shank, Greenville, North Carolina; Chuck Shepherd, Washington, D.C.; Jim Springer, Kettering, Ohio; Bill Steckman, West Hempstead, New York; Mario Tedeschi, Rome; Edward Thorpe, Newport Beach, California; Susan Timper, Pan Am World Airways, New York; Filippo Todini, Assisi; Samuel W. Valenza, Jr., *Lottery Player's Magazine*, Moorestown, New Jersey; David Van der Meulem, University of Virginia, Charlottesville; Virginia State Lottery, Fairfax; Bob Vogel, Mesa, Arizona; Rich Wardell, Special Investigations, Meriden State Police, Meriden, Connecticut; Michael Wayne, Batjac Productions, Beverly Hills, California; H. Ellen Whitely, Amarillo, Texas.

PICTURE CREDITS

The sources for the illustrations that appear in this book are listed below. Credits from left to right are separated by semicolons, from top to bottom by dashes.

Cover: Michael P. Gadomski/Bruce Coleman, New York, background, Fil Hunter. **3:** Michael P. Gadomski/Bruce Coleman, New York. **7:** Art Resource, New York, background, Pelton & Associates, Inc./Westlight, Los Angeles. **8:** Courtesy of the Trustees of the British Museum, London. **9:** Gianni Dagli Orti, Paris. **10:** British Library, London; courtesy of the Trustees of the British Museum, London. **11:** Pedicini, Naples. **12:** The United States Playing Card Company Museum, Cincinnati (2); Roger-Viollet, Paris—courtesy of the Trustees of the Victoria and Albert Museum, London (3). **13:** Deutsches Spielkarten-Museum, Leinfelden-Echterdingen. **14:** National Portrait Gallery, London. **15:** From *Giacomo Casanova und sein Lebensroman*, by Gustav

Gugitz, Verlag Ed. Strache, Wein, 1921; Arizona State Museum, Tucson (4). **16:** Archives de la Société des Baines de Mer, Monte Carlo; the Mansell Collection, London. **17:** Library of Congress LC-104763; C. Phillips for *LIFE*. **18:** Denver Public Library, Western History Department, Denver. **19:** From *Knights of the Green Cloth: The Saga of the Frontier Gamblers*, by Robert K. DeArment, University of Oklahoma Press, Norman, 1982. **20:** Denver Public Library, Western History Department, Denver. **21:** The Mansell Collection, London. **22:** Culver Pictures, New York. **23:** The Bettmann Archive, New York. **24:** The Bettmann Archive, New York; Culver Pictures, New York. **25:** The Hulton Picture Company, London. **26, 27:** Culver Pictures, New York; FPG, New York. **28:** Courtesy Time Inc. Magazines Picture Collection, New York. **29:** UPI/Bettmann, New York. **30, 31:** Culver Pictures, New York. **32:** Richard Nixon Library and Birthplace, Yorba Linda, California. **33:** UPI/

Bettmann, New York. **34, 35:** Leigh Wiener. **36:** Binion's Horseshoe Hotel, Las Vegas. **37:** Neal Preston. **39:** Evan Sheppard, background, Robert Landau/Westlight, Los Angeles. **40:** Library of Congress (2); AP/Wide World Photos, New York; Alfred Eisenstaedt for *LIFE*. **41:** British Library, London. **42:** Bally Manufacturing Corporation, Chicago; the Society of Antiquaries, London. **43:** Edimedia, Paris. **44:** The Hulton Picture Company, London. **45:** LGI © 1985, New York. **46:** Ron Karafin/*Courier-Post*, Cherry Hill, New Jersey. **47:** Evan Sheppard. **48:** John Green/UPI Bettmann Newsphotos, New York— New Jersey State Lottery, Trenton. **49:** Courtesy Palace Station Hotel-Casino, Las Vegas. **50:** Shane Kelley/*Montreal Gazette*, Montreal—Evan Sheppard. **51:** Cheung Ching Ming/*PEOPLE* Weekly. **52:** Detroit Free Press, Inc., Detroit. **53:** Michael Mercanti/*Philadelphia Daily News*, Philadelphia. **54:** Evan Sheppard. **55:** Edimedia, Paris; Lauros-Giraudon, Paris. **56:** Istituto

by Carol Belanger Grafton, Dover Publications, Inc., New York, 1988 (1)—from *Animals: 1419 Copyright-Free Illustrations*, selected by Jim Harter, Dover Publications, Inc., New York, 1979 (3). **111:** Charr Crail/*The Press Tribune*, Roseville, California. **113:** The Granger Collection, New York, background, R. Clevenger/Westlight, Los Angeles. **114:** University of Texas, El Paso, Library Special Collections, El Paso, Texas. **115:** D. Gorton/*Time*. **116:** The design of the certificates is Crown copyright and is reproduced with the permission of the controller of HMSO; D. J. Page, Mitcham, Surrey, England. **117:** Craig Herndon/*The Washington Post*, Washington, D.C. **118:** British Library, London. **119:** Mary Evans Picture Library, London. **120:** Parks College of St. Louis University, Cahokia, Illinois. **121:** Biomedical Communications Division, the Ohio State University Archives, Columbus, Ohio. **122:** The Hulton Picture Company, London. **123:** Giancarlo Costa, Milan. **124:** The Granger Collection, New York. **125:** The Bettmann Archive, New York. **126:** Jean-Loup Charmet, Paris. **127:** The Bettmann Archive, New York. **128:** Jean-Loup Charmet, Paris. **129:** Popperfoto, London—Library of Congress LC-8244797. **130:** The Granger Collection, New York—J. Bryan, III. **131:** The Granger Collection, New York. **132, 133:** Culver Pictures, New York.

BIBLIOGRAPHY

Books

Allen, David D. *The Nature of Gambling.* New York: Coward-McCann, 1952.

Ambrose, Stephen E. *Nixon.* New York: Simon & Schuster, 1987.

Arnold, Peter:
 The Encyclopedia of Gambling. Secaucus, N.J.: Chartwell Books, 1977.
 Gambling. London: Hamlyn, 1974.

Asbury, Herbert. *Sucker's Progress.* New York: Dodd, Mead, 1938.

Ashley, Leonard R. N. *The Wonderful World of Superstition, Prophecy and Luck.* New York: Dembner Books, 1984.

Bach, Richard. *Nothing by Chance: A Gypsy Pilot's Adventures in Modern America.* New York: William Morrow, 1969.

Barnhart, Clarence L., and William D. Halsey (Eds.). *The New Century Cyclopedia of Names* (Vol. 1). New York: Appleton-Century-Crofts, 1954.

Barnhart, Russell T. *Gamblers of Yesteryear.* Las Vegas, Nev.: Press, 1983.

Brackman, Arnold C. *The Search for the Gold of Tutankhamen.* New York: Mason/Charter, 1976.

Bradshaw, Jon. *Fast Company.* New York: Harper & Row, 1975.

Brenner, Reuven, and Gabrielle A. Brenner. *Gambling and Speculation: A Theory, a History, and a Future of Some Human Decisions.* Cambridge: Cambridge University Press, 1990.

Bryan, J., III. *The Sword over the Mantel.* New York: McGraw-Hill, 1960.

Budge, E. A. Wallis. *Amulets and Superstitions.* New York: Dover, 1978.

Cavendish, Richard (Ed.). *Encyclopedia of the Unexplained.* New York: McGraw-Hill, 1974.

Clotfelter, Charles T., and Philip J. Cook. *Selling Hope: State Lotteries in America.* Cambridge, Mass.: Harvard University Press, 1989.

Cohen, Daniel. *The Encyclopedia of the Strange.* New York: Dodd, Mead, 1985.

Costello, William. *The Facts about Nixon.* New York: Viking Press, 1960.

Daniels, Cora Linn, and C. M. Stevans (Eds.). *Encyclopædia of Superstitions, Folklore, and the Occult Sciences of the World* (Vol. 3). Detroit: Gale Research, Book Tower, 1971 (reprint of 1903 edition).

David, F. N. *Games, Gods and Gambling.* New York: Hafner, 1962.

DeArment, Robert K. *Knights of the Green Cloth: The Saga of the Frontier Gamblers.* Norman: University of Oklahoma Press, 1982.

Devol, George H. *Forty Years a Gambler on the Mississippi.* Cincinnati: Devol & Haines, 1887.

Distasi, Lawrence. *Mal Occhio [Evil Eye]: The Underside of Vision.* San Francisco: North Point Press, 1981.

Drago, Harry Sinclair. *Notorious Ladies of the Frontier.* New York: Dodd, Mead, 1969.

Dummett, Michael, and Sylvia Mann. *The Game of Tarot.* London: Duckworth, 1980.

Dundes, Alan. *Interpreting Folklore.* Bloomington: Indiana University Press, 1980.

Eadington, William R. *Gambling and Society.* Springfield, Ill.: Charles C Thomas, 1976.

Earp, Wyatt S. *Wyatt Earp.* Sierra Vista, Ariz.: Yoma V. Bissette, 1981.

Eichler, Lillian. *The Customs of Mankind.* Garden City, N.Y.: Nelson Doubleday, 1924.

Encyclopaedia Judaica (Vol. 7). Jerusalem:

Keter, 1971.

Ewen, C. L'Estrange. *Lotteries and Sweepstakes.* New York: Benjamin Blom, 1972.

Ezell, John Samuel. *Fortune's Merry Wheel: The Lottery in America.* Cambridge, Mass.: Harvard University Press, 1960.

Facts & Fallacies. Pleasantville, N.Y.: Reader's Digest Association, 1988.

Fehrenbach, T. R. *Comanches: The Destruction of a People.* New York: Alfred A. Knopf, 1974.

Findlay, John M. *People of Chance.* New York: Oxford University Press, 1986.

Flammarion, Camille. *L'Inconnu: The Unknown.* New York: Harper & Brothers, 1900.

Fleming, Alice. *Something for Nothing.* New York: Delacorte Press, 1978.

Funk & Wagnalls Standard Dictionary of Folklore, Mythology, and Legend. San Francisco: Harper & Row, 1972.

Gaddis, Vincent. *Invisible Horizons: True Mysteries of the Sea.* Philadelphia: Chilton Books, 1965.

Gill, Brendan. *Tallulah.* New York: Holt, Rinehart & Winston, 1972.

Gillispie, Charles Coulston (Ed.). *Dictionary of Scientific Biography* (Vol. 3). New York: Charles Scribner's Sons, 1971.

Godley, John. *Tell Me the Next One.* London: Victor Gollancz, 1950.

Goff, John S. *Robert Todd Lincoln: A Man in His Own Right.* Norman: University of Oklahoma Press, 1969.

Graham, J. A. Maxtone. *Eccentric Gamblers* (Mowbrays Eccentrics series). London: Mowbrays, 1975.

Graves, Charles. *None But the Rich.* London: Cassell, 1963.

Gunther, Max. *The Luck Factor.* New York: Macmillan, 1977.

Hardy, Alister, Robert Harvie, and Arthur Koestler. *The Challenge of Chance.* New York: Random House, 1973.

Hargrave, Catherine Perry. *A History of Playing Cards and a Bibliography of Cards and Gaming.* New York: Dover, 1966.

Haskins, James. *Pinckney Benton Stewart Pinchback.* New York: Macmillan, 1973.

Hay, Peter. *Theatrical Anecdotes.* New York: Oxford University Press, 1987.

Hayano, David M. *Poker Faces.* Berkeley: University of California Press, 1982.

Herald, George W., and Edward D. Radin. *The Big Wheel.* New York: William Morrow, 1963.

Hinds, Alfred. *Contempt of Court.* London: Bodley Head, 1966.

Horan, James D. *The Pinkertons.* New York: Crown, 1967.

Huff, Darrell. *How to Take a Chance.* New York: W. W. Norton, 1959.

Huggett, Richard:

The Curse of Macbeth: And Other Theatrical Superstitions. Chippenham, Wiltshire: Picton, 1981.

Supernatural on Stage: Ghosts and Superstitions of the Theatre. New York: Taplinger, 1975.

Hutchens, John K. (Ed.). *The Gambler's Bedside Book.* New York: Taplinger, 1977.

Jahoda, Gustav. *The Psychology of Superstition.* London: Allen Lane The Penguin Press, 1969.

James, Marquis. *Andrew Jackson.* New York: Grosset & Dunlap, 1933.

Katcher, Leo. *The Big Bankroll: The Life and Times of Arnold Rothstein.* New York: Harper & Brothers, 1958.

Kopper, Philip. *The National Museum of Natural History.* New York: Harry N. Abrams, 1982.

Lasker, Edward:

Go and Go-Moku: The Oriental Board Games and Their American Versions. New York: Alfred A. Knopf, 1934.

Modern Chess Strategy. Philadelphia: David McKay, 1945.

Laughlin, Ruth. *The Wind Leaves No Shadow.* Caldwell, Idaho: Caxton Printers, 1951.

Longstreet, Stephen. *Win or Lose.* Indianapolis: Bobbs-Merrill, 1977.

Ludovici, L. J. *The Itch for Play.* London: Jarrolds, 1962.

Lys, Claudia De. *A Treasury of Superstitions.* New York: Philosophical Library, 1957.

Lyttle, Richard B. *The Games They Played.* New York: Atheneum, 1982.

McCullough, David W. *Brooklyn—and How It Got That Way.* New York: Dial Press, 1983.

MacDougall, Curtis D. *Superstition and the Press.* Buffalo, N.Y.: Prometheus Books, 1983.

McGervey, John D. *Probabilities in Everyday Life.* Chicago: Nelson-Hall, 1986.

Maloney, Clarence (Ed.). *The Evil Eye.* New York: Columbia University Press, 1976.

Mann, Sylvia. *Collecting Playing Cards.* New York: Crown, 1966.

Maple, Eric. *Superstition and the Superstitious.* Cranbury, N.J.: A. S. Barnes, 1972.

Mayer, L. A. *Mamluk Playing Cards.* Edited by R. Ettinghausen and O. Kurz. Leiden: E. J. Brill, 1971.

Messick, Hank, and Burt Goldblatt. *The Only Game in Town.* New York: Thomas Y. Crowell, 1976.

Michell, John, and Robert J. M. Rickard. *Phenomena: A Book of Wonders.* New York: Pantheon Books, 1977.

Morley, Christopher. "Preface." In *Boswell's London Journal, 1762-1763,* by James Boswell. New York: McGraw-Hill, 1951.

Mysteries of the Unexplained. Pleasantville, N.Y.: Reader's Digest Association, 1982.

Narasimhan, Chakravarthi V. *The Mahābhārata.* New York: Columbia University Press, 1965.

The New Encyclopædia Britannica (Vols. 4, 7, 9). Chicago: Encyclopædia Britannica, 1985.

Nicolson, Harold. *Small Talk.* New York: Harcourt, Brace, 1937.

Nixon, Richard. *The Memoirs of Richard Nixon.* New York: Grosset & Dunlap, 1978.

Nouët, Noël. *Histoire de Tokyo.* Paris: Presses Universitaires de France, 1961.

O'Connor, Richard. *Wild Bill Hickok.* Garden City, N.Y.: Doubleday, 1959.

Ore, Oystein. *Cardano: The Gambling Scholar.* Princeton, N.J.: Princeton University Press, 1953.

Panati, Charles. *Extraordinary Origins of Everyday Things.* New York: Harper & Row, 1987.

Park, Edwards. *Treasures of the Smithsonian.* Washington, D.C.: Smithsonian Books, 1983.

Patch, Susanne Steinem. *Blue Mystery: The Story of the Hope Diamond.* Washington, D.C.: Smithsonian Institution Press, 1976.

Paulos, John Allen. *Innumeracy: Mathematical Illiteracy and Its Consequences.* New York: Farrar, Straus & Giroux, Hill & Wang, 1988.

Perl, Lila. *Don't Sing before Breakfast, Don't Sleep in the Moonlight.* New York: Clarion Books, 1988.

Pottle, Frederick A. "The History of the Boswell Papers." In *Boswell's London Journal, 1762-1763,* by James Boswell. New York: McGraw-Hill, 1951.

Quinn, John Philip. *Fools of Fortune: Or Gambling and Gamblers.* Chicago: G. L. Howe, 1890.

Rachleff, Owen S. *The Secrets of Superstitions: How They Help, How They Hurt.* Garden City, N.Y.: Doubleday, 1976.

Radford, Edwin, and M. A. Radford. *Encyclopædia of Superstitions.* Westport, Conn.: Greenwood Press, 1969.

Remini, Robert V. *Andrew Jackson.* New York: Harper & Row, 1966.

Rice, Cy. *Nick the Greek.* New York: Funk & Wagnalls, 1969.

Richards, Steve. *Luck, Chance & Coincidence.* San Bernardino, Calif.: Borgo Press, 1988.

Ripley's Believe It or Not! Book of Chance. Toronto: Ripley Books, 1982.

Roberts, Randy, and James S. Olson. *Winning Is the Only Thing.* Baltimore: Johns Hopkins University Press, 1989.

Rossbach, Sarah. *Interior Design with Feng Shui.* New York: E. P. Dutton, 1987.

Shepherd, Chuck, John J. Kohut, and Roland Sweet. *News of the Weird.* New York: Penguin Books, New American Library, 1989.

Sifakis, Carl. *American Eccentrics.* New York:

Facts On File, 1984.

Sothern, Edward H. *The Melancholy Tale of "Me": My Remembrances.* New York: Charles Scribner's Sons, 1916.

Steinmetz, Andrew. *The Gaming Table: Its Votaries and Victims.* Montclair, N.J.: Patterson Smith, 1969.

Stoddard, Lothrop. *Luck: Your Silent Partner.* New York: Horace Liveright, 1929.

Stouffer, Samuel A., et al. *The American Soldier: Combat and Its Aftermath* (Vol. 2). Princeton, N.J.: Princeton University Press, 1949.

Strange Stories, Amazing Facts. Pleasantville, N.Y.: Reader's Digest Association, 1976.

Sullivan, George:
   By Chance a Winner: The History of Lotteries. New York: Dodd, Mead, 1972.
   Sports Superstitions. New York: Coward, McCann & Geoghegan, 1978.

Swanson, Leslie C. *Riverboat Gamblers of History.* Moline, Ill.: Leslie C. Swanson, 1989.

Thackrey, Ted, Jr. *Gambling Secrets of Nick the Greek.* Chicago: Rand McNally, 1968.

Thompson, C. J. S. *The Hand of Destiny: Folklore and Superstition for Everyday Life.* New York: Bell, 1989.

Thorp, Edward O.:
   Beat the Dealer: A Winning Strategy for the Game of Twenty-One. New York: Random House, Blaisdell, 1962.
   The Mathematics of Gambling. Hollywood: Gambling Times, 1984.

Tredd, William E. *Dice Games: New and Old.* Cambridge: Oleander Press, 1981.

Tuleja, Tad. *Curious Customs.* New York: Stonesong Press, 1987.

Vaughan, Alan. *Incredible Coincidence.* New York: J. B. Lippincott, 1979.

Wagman, Robert. *Instant Millionaires.* Kensington, Md.: Woodbine House, 1986.

Walker, Barbara G. *The Woman's Encyclopedia of Myths and Secrets.* San Francisco: Harper & Row, 1983.

Wallace, Irving, David Wallechinsky, and Amy Wallace. *Significa.* New York: E. P. Dutton, 1983.

Wallechinsky, David, and Irving Wallace. *The People's Almanac.* Garden City, N.Y.: Doubleday, 1975.

Watson, Peter. *Twins: An Uncanny Relationship?* New York: Viking Press, 1981.

Weaver, Warren. *Lady Luck: The Theory of Probability.* Garden City, N.Y.: Doubleday, Anchor Books, 1963.

Williams, Roger L. *Gaslight and Shadow: The World of Napoleon III, 1851-1870.* New York: Macmillan, 1957.

Willison, George F. *Behold Virginia: The Fifth Crown.* New York: Harcourt, Brace, 1951.

Woollcott, Alexander. *While Rome Burns.* New York: Viking Press, 1934.

Wowk, Kathleen. *Playing Cards of the World.* Guildford, Surrey: Lutterworth Press, 1983.

Wykes, Alan. *The Complete Illustrated Guide to Gambling.* Garden City, N.Y.: Doubleday, 1964.

Young, Thomas. *An Account of Some Recent Discoveries in Hieroglyphical Literature, and Egyptian Antiquities.* London: John Murray, 1823.

Periodicals

Allison, Renee. "Surgery Reveals Diamond, Not Cancer." *Roseville Press Tribune,* October 25, 1988.

Allston, Tom. "Dog Returns Home after 750-Mile Odyssey." *Amarillo Adventure,* June 10, 1987.

"As Chance Would Have It." *Time,* April 14, 1986.

"Astonishing Alfie." *London Daily Mail,* July 30, 1964.

Ball, Don. "Lottery Rich Man Faces Drug Charge." *Detroit News,* October 27, 1984.

Barrett, Cindy, and Bruce Wallace. "Sharing the Windfall." *Maclean's,* April 14, 1986.

Bayer, Amy. "Are Lotteries a Ripoff?" *Consumers' Research,* January 1990.

Beam, Roger. "Spend, Spend, Spend an Evening with Me!" *London Daily Mirror,* June 22, 1978.

"Beatrice Church Demolished." *Nebraska State Journal,* March 3, 1950.

Beck, Melinda, et al. "The Lottery Craze." *Newsweek,* September 2, 1985.

Birnbaum, Ken. "The Hero Returns to Hugs, Praise: Toddler's Rescuer Is Shy in Limelight." *The Record* (Northern New Jersey), May 3, 1989.

Blake, Gene. "Can Courts Apply Theory of Probability to Cases?" *Los Angeles Times,* October 20, 1967.

"Blast Levels Beatrice Church Just before Choir's Assembly." *Nebraska State Journal,* March 2, 1950.

Blodgett, Richard. "Our Wild, Weird World of Coincidence." *Reader's Digest,* September 1987.

Blum, Harold. "Troubles Plague Train to New York." *New York Times,* August 26, 1983.

Blumenthal, Ralph. "Subway Offers a Glimpse of Far Horizons." *New York Times,* December 23, 1977.

Boldenweck, Bill, and Julia Day. "Stolen Chinese Statues Recovered." *San Francisco Examiner,* August 21, 1986.

Browning, E. S. "When Fung Shui Speaks, Business Listens." *International Wildlife,* September-October 1984.

Bryan, J., III. "A Certain Concurrence of Circumstances." *Holiday,* November 1962.

Cambareri, Carmen S. "The Herman Melville Papers." *American History Illustrated,* October 1984.

Camel, Jeffrey J. "The History That Hides behind the Surface of a Painting." *Christian Science Monitor,* February 15, 1984.

Chesley, Richard:
   " 'Like a Dream': Sisters Reunited behind Bars." *The State* (Columbia, S.C.), November 6, 1988.
   "Reunited Sisters Connect with Lost Brother in Prison." *The State* (Columbia, S.C.), November 16, 1988.
   "Two Sisters Who Met behind Bars Discover Half Brother in Columbia." *The State* (Columbia, S.C.), November 8, 1988.

Chua-Eoan, Howard G. "How to Keep the Dragons Happy." *Time,* June 22, 1987.

Clark, Joe. "First He's Healthy, and Now He's Wealthy." *Philadelphia Daily News,* September 23, 1983.

Cohen, Jerry. "Law of Probability Helps Convict Couple." *Los Angeles Times,* December 11, 1964.

Coleman, Jane. "Gamblin' Man." *Alaska,* May 1990.

Conrad, Barnaby. "A Woeful Gallery of the World's Lost Masterpieces." *Smithsonian,* November 1987.

Conrad, Eric. "Jersey Couple Claim $15.3 Million Jackpot." *The Patriot,* July 27, 1988.

Curtis, Charlotte. "The Melville Treasures." *New York Times,* July 12, 1983.

Dallos, Robert E. "It's No Day to Ask How Business Is." *Los Angeles Times,* April 13, 1979.

Dawson, James P. "LaMotta Indefinitely Suspended for Concealing Side Injury before Fox Bout." *New York Times,* November 22, 1947.

Dawson, Jim. "7000 B.C.: A Hunter-Gatherer Walked This Land." *Star Tribune,* July 27, 1990.

"Death of Local Actor after 'Macbeth' Stabbing Incident." *Oldham Standard,* March 1, 1947.

"Detectives' Convention Stymied Shoplifters." *Barnsley Chronicle,* February 9, 1979.

Dillard, Gene. "Former NY Winner Claims NJ Lotto Jackpot." *Lottery Player's Magazine,* June 1990.

"District Attorney Opens Fight Inquiry." *New York Times,* November 20, 1947.

Donovan, Richard, and Hank Greenspun:
   "Nick the Greek: Fabulous King of the Gamblers." *Collier's,* April 2, 1954.
   "Of Dice and Men." *Collier's,* April 30, 1954.

Dougherty, Margaret, and Dirk Mathison. "Out of the Ashes, a Family Restored." *People,* February 13, 1989.

Edeal, George H. "Why the Choir Was Late." *Life,*

March 27, 1950.

Escobar, Gariel. "Disputed Lotto Jackpot Big Enough for All Once Judge Figures the Split." *Philadelphia Daily News*, November 10, 1988.

" 'Fantasy' Comes True." *Chicago Tribune*, July 1, 1983.

"Faster than a Speeding Bullet, Anthony Falzo Saved Two Tots from a Powerful Locomotive." *People*, May 22, 1989.

Ferrell, David. "Cat's Tale Ends Happily." *Los Angeles Times*, January 22, 1988.

"$15.3 Million Catch That Almost Got Away." *New York Times*, July 27, 1988.

"Final Appeal Lost by Lotto 'Winner.' " *New York Times*, May 4, 1983.

"Five Husbands and £150,000 Later." *Guardian*, March 3, 1977.

"$4.4 Million Win in Lotto Helps Cancer Victim." *Philadelphia Inquirer*, September 23, 1983.

Friedman, Jack. "The Most Peppery Game since the Stove League? It's Rotisserie Baseball." *People*, April 23, 1984.

Galen, Michele. "A Chinese Art for Changing Your Fortune." *Business Week*, August 6, 1990.

Gallagher, Maria:

"Jury: Pair Must Split Disputed $4.4M Lotto." *Philadelphia Daily News*, August 31, 1988.

"Winnings His Alone, Jury Told: $4.4 Million Winner Denies Split Claim." *Philadelphia Daily News*, August 27, 1988.

Gardner, Martin:

"It's More Probable than You Think." *Reader's Digest*, November 1967.

"Mathematical Games." *American*, October 1972.

George, Ron. "God or Garfield?" *Corpus Christi Caller*, September 19, 1989.

"Getting Even." *Newsweek*, October 21, 1985.

"Glimpses of the Past." *Sporting News*, October 16, 1989.

Goldstein, Steve. "Superstitious?" *World Tennis*, February 1988.

Goss, Michael. "The Ring-in-the-Fish Story." *Fate*, April 1987.

Grogan, David. "After 24 Years Pushing Pizza, Waitress Phyllis Penzo Gets a Tip to Remember: $3 Million." *People*, April 23, 1984.

Hackett, Larry. "Lucky Strike: The Series." *Daily News*, March 30, 1990.

Haitch, Richard. "$3 Million 'Tip.' " *New York Times*, October 28, 1984.

Hardy, Thomas. "Firm May Pay Peoria Man $100,000 in Lottery Misprint." *Chicago Tribune*, June 3, 1983.

Hoffman, Paul. "*Triskaidekaphobia* Can Strike When You're Most Expecting It." *Smithsonian*, February 1987.

Hoffman, Ray. "Playing Ball with Stats—Not

Bats." *Business Week*, May 14, 1990.

"Hub Museum Uncovers Long-Lost Millet Work." *Providence Journal*, January 31, 1989.

Hughes, Robert. "Empirical Queen of the Sciences." *Time*, October 14, 1974.

"The Illegal Millionaire." *Time*, November 18, 1985.

"Ill-Fated Amtrak Train Hit by More Misfortune." *Washington Post*, August 27, 1983.

" 'I Love It,' Shouts New Millionaire." *Detroit News*, August 6, 1975.

Ireland, Tim. "The $4-Million Man Keeps on Winning . . ." *The Trentonian*, March 28, 1990.

"Italian Premier Resigns in Dispute Arising from Palestinian Hijacking of Cruise Ship." *Facts On File*, October 18, 1985.

"Jackpot Claimed as Time Runs Out." *The Patriot*, July 16, 1988.

Jarman, Rufus. "The Great Racetrack Caper." *American Heritage*, August 1968.

Jarvis, Birney. "Ex-Wife Blew the Whistle on Theft." *San Francisco Chronicle*, August 22, 1986.

Jenks, Albert Ernest. "Minnesota's Browns Valley Man and Associated Burial Artifacts." *American Anthropological Association*, 1937, Memoirs, 49.

Johnson, Ben E. "Wanna Bet?" *TWA Ambassador*, July 1990.

Kaplan, Morris. "Empire State Leap Ends on 85th Floor." *New York Times*, December 24, 1977.

Kaufman, Michael T. "Pearl Harbor Attack Is Linked to Ads." *New York Times*, March 12, 1967.

Kelly, Roberta House. "The Box." *Southern Living*, December 1987.

Kerwin, Katie. "2-Year-Old Survives 3-Story Fall." *Rocky Mountain News*, October 11, 1989.

King, Jonathon, and Valeria M. Russ. "Cops: $4M Put Bounce in His Step." *Philadelphia Daily News*, June 8, 1984.

Kiska, Tim. "Life Wasn't All Roses after the Lottery Million." *Detroit Free Press*, October 28, 1964.

Koestler, Arthur:

"Beyond Our Understanding." *London Sunday Times*, November 25, 1973.

"The Mysterious Power of Chance." *London Sunday Times*, May 4, 1974.

Koncius, Jura. "If It Feels Good, It Could Be Feng Shui." *Washington Post*, March 21, 1991.

"LaMotta Confesses He Threw '47 Garden Bout with Billy Fox." *New York Times*, June 15, 1960.

Lerner, Steve. "The Gansevoort Papers." *Connoisseur*, May 1985.

"Life's a Gamble." *Grand Rapids Press*, February 8, 1989.

Link, Terry. "Notorious Art Theft Was a Teenage Prank." *The Tribune*, August 22, 1986.

"Living Well Is the Best Revenge." *Newsweek*, September 2, 1985.

Loflin, Alan. "Felix the Cat Logs 180,000 Miles in December." *Pan-Am Clipper*, February 1988.

"Lotteries: Even Winners Are Lucky to Break Even." *Money*, November 1988.

Lottman, Herbert R. "Madrid's Great Leonardo Discovery Inspires a Major McGraw-Hill Co-publishing Project." *Publishers Weekly*, May 27, 1974.

"Lotto Jackpot Winner Given Probation in Bad-Check Case." *Philadelphia Inquirer*, August 22, 1984.

"Lotto Ray Gets Lucky in Court." *Philadelphia Daily News*, June 27, 1985.

"Lotto Winner Is to Be Tried in Worthless Checks Case." *Philadelphia Inquirer*, August 17, 1984.

McCallum, Jack. "Green Cats, Black Cats & Lady Luck." *Sports Illustrated*, February 8, 1988.

McCoy, Ronald. "Apache Rawhide Playing Cards." *American Indian Art*, Summer 1984.

McKinney, Rhoda E. "Has Money Spoiled the Lottery Millionaires?" *Ebony*, December 1988.

Macnow, Glen. "How to Win $1 Million and Ruin Your Life." *Detroit Free Press*, December 16, 1984.

Makeig, John. "Judge Again Jails Suspect." *Houston Chronicle*, November 2, 1989.

"Man Pleads Guilty." *Detroit Free Press*, February 26, 1985.

"Mr. Harold Norman Dies in Infirmary Month after Theatre Stabbing Accident." *Oldham Evening Chronicle*, February 26, 1947.

Moore, Trudy S. "Learning to Live with $5 Million." *Ebony*, April 1983.

"1947 Fight Story Indicated a 'Fix.' " *New York Times*, June 15, 1960.

Norman, Bud. "Dating Couple Learn They Share a Father." *Wichita Eagle Beacon*, May 13, 1988.

Odom, Maida. "Lotto Winner Again Faces Check Charges." *Philadelphia Inquirer*, August 29, 1984.

O'Flaherty, Michael. "Hinds: I Demand a New Trial." *Daily Mail*, July 30, 1954.

Ola, Per, and Emily D'Aulaire. "Chain of Circumstance." *Reader's Digest*, December 1987.

O'Neil, Paul. "The Professor Who Breaks the Bank." *Life*, March 27, 1964.

Pick, Grant. "When They First Dated, These Two Kansans Felt a Strong Attraction to Each Other; Now They Know Why." *People*, June 13, 1988.

Platteborze, Walt. "Girl 'Hero' Is Safely Home;

Playmate Still Hospitalized." *New Haven Register,* February 22, 1987.

"Pool Men Beaten at Last." *New York Times,* September 16, 1891.

"Prosecutor's Aides Question LaMotta." *New York Times,* November 21, 1947.

Rein, Richard K. "The Lottery Game." *Money,* November 1984.

"Relics of Wreck." *Life,* May 18, 1953.

Romero, Lorenzo P.:

"His Luck May Be Running Out." *San Jose Mercury News,* November 6, 1985.

"Lottery Winner Is 'Same Jose.'" *San Jose Mercury News,* January 20, 1986.

Rosenthal, Gloria. "The Robe with a Past . . . and a Future." *Patient's Digest,* 1984, Vol. 1, no. 2.

Ross, Irwin. "Corporate Winners in the Lottery Boom." *Fortune,* September 3, 1984.

Rubin, Neal. "At Home on Easy Street." *Detroit Free Press,* November 10, 1987.

Russell, Edith. "I Was Aboard the *Titanic.*" *Ladies Home Companion,* May 1964.

Sarbaugh, Donald. "Homeless Man Who Slept on Scrap Paper Hits $2.7 Million Jackpot." *National Enquirer,* February 28, 1989.

Schumacher, Geoff. "Former Street Person Wins $2.76M Jackpot." *Las Vegas Sun,* February 7, 1989.

Sharpe, Martyn. " 'Spend, Spend' Viv Was Saved by Drug SOS." *The Sun,* February 6, 1978.

"Shuffling into Hyperspace." *Discover,* January 1991.

Skow, John. "The Big Poker Freeze-Out." *Time,* June 18, 1990.

Smallwood, LaViece. "A Real-Life Story of Love and Abiding Memories." *Florida Times-Union,* December 24, 1989.

Sokolove, Michael. "$4.4M Winner Found Fame, Lost Fortune." *Philadelphia Daily News,* October 8, 1984.

" 'Spend, Spend' Wife's Fifth Husband Dies." *Daily Telegraph,* October 10, 1975.

"State Says City's 'Instant' Lottery Winner to Receive $100,000 in About a Month." *Journal*

Star, June 3, 1983.

Stevens, Joann. "Wanda, Wanda." *Washington Post,* April 20, 1978.

Stix, Harriet. "Triplets to Reunite after 57 Years." *Los Angeles Times,* July 14, 1983.

Stone, Gene. "Games." *Playboy,* June 1988.

Sturgis, Chris. "60-Year Separation Ends for Mom, Son." *Binghamton Press & Sun-Bulletin,* January 18, 1989.

Stutz, Howard. "Heading for Easy Street." *Las Vegas Review-Journal,* February 7, 1989.

"Sudermann Dies, 71; Noted Dramatist." *New York Times,* November 22, 1928.

Sullivan, Walter:

"Science: More on Leonardo." *New York Times,* February 19, 1967.

"700 Pages of Leonardo MSS. Found in Madrid." *New York Times,* February 14, 1967.

"Swampscott, Cash Short, Eying a Long Shot." *New York Times,* May 4, 1986.

"They Are Caught at Last." *New York Times,* September 26, 1891.

"$3 Million 'Tip' for Yonkers Waitress." *New York Times,* April 3, 1984.

"Too Much for Pool Men." *New York Times,* September 18, 1891.

Totzauer, Josef, and Allen Rankin. "Love at First Sound." *Reader's Digest,* October 1989.

"Toy Protection." *Philadelphia Inquirer,* September 24, 1989.

"Trails: The Laws of Probability." *Time,* January 8, 1965.

Trefil, James. "Odds Are against Your Breaking That Law of Averages." *Smithsonian,* September 1984.

"Trial by Mathematics." *Time,* April 26, 1968.

"Troubled Amtrak Train in a New Accident." *New York Times,* August 27, 1983.

Turner, Jonathan. "Perugia: A Rediscovered Raphael." *ARTnews,* April 1990.

Turner, Robert, and Kevin Cosgrove. "Now Spend-Spend Vivien Loses Husband No 5." *Daily Mail,* October 10, 1975.

"Two Break into San Quentin." *Rock Island Argus,* September 29, 1989.

"2 Charged in Drug Case Revealed by Wrong Number." *Kansas City Times,* November 21, 1986.

"Two Lives—A Weird Coincidence." *San Francisco Chronicle,* April 22, 1978.

"2-Year-Old Survives Fall." *Gwinnett Daily News,* October 12, 1989.

"What Made Elvita Jump?" *New York Daily News,* December 1, 1979.

Wilson, Robert A. "Mere Coincidence?" *Science Digest,* January 1982.

"The Winners of Quebec's Largest Lottery Prove that Honesty Is the Best-Paying Policy." *People,* April 21, 1986.

Wulf, Steve. "First Person." *Sports Illustrated,* May 14, 1984.

Ziegler, Edward. "Coincidence: Is It Black Magic or Blind Chance?" *Reader's Digest,* August 1979.

Other Sources

Brown, Elizabeth, and Bonnie Nelson Schwartz. "The Gypsy Robe's Enduring Mystique." Helen Hayes Awards Program. Washington, D.C.: John F. Kennedy Center, May 4, 1987.

Butturini, Paula. "Ship-Troubles." News release. Rome: UPI, October 8, 1985.

"Drugbust." News release. Kansas City, Mo.: UPI, November 21, 1986.

"Eusebius, Historia Ecclesiastica, in the Latin Translation of Rufinus, a Decorated Bifolium from a Manuscript on Vellum." Sotheby's London Catalog. London: July 25, 1985.

"Jean-Francois Millet Exhibition at the Museum of Fine Arts, Boston, March 28 through July 1, 1984." Press release. Boston: Museum of Fine Arts, January 6, 1984.

"Lotto Lightning Strikes Again for Hunterdon County Couple." Press release. Trenton, N.J.: New Jersey State Lottery, March 27, 1990.

McClellan, Rachel. "The Boswell Office." Presentation given October 1989. Yale University.

Murphy, Alexandra R. "Jean-François Millet." Exhibition Catalog. Boston: Museum of Fine Arts, 1984.

INDEX

Numbers in italics indicate an illustration of the subject mentioned.

142

Time-Life Books is a division of Time Life Inc.,
a wholly owned subsidiary of
THE TIME INC. BOOK COMPANY

TIME-LIFE BOOKS

Managing Editor: Thomas H. Flaherty
Director of Editorial Resources:
Elise D. Ritter-Clough
Director of Photography and Research:
John Conrad Weiser
Editorial Board: Dale M. Brown, Roberta Conlan,
Laura Foreman, Lee Hassig, Jim Hicks,
Blaine Marshall, Rita Thievon Mullin, Henry
Woodhead

PUBLISHER: Joseph J. Ward

Associate Publisher: Ann M. Mirabito
Editorial Director: Russell B. Adams, Jr.
Marketing Director: Anne C. Everhart
Director of Design: Louis Klein
Production Manager: Prudence G. Harris
Supervisor of Quality Control: James King

Editorial Operations
Production: Celia Beattie
Library: Louise D. Forstall
Computer Composition: Deborah G. Tait (Manager),
Monika D. Thayer, Janet Barnes Syring,
Lillian Daniels

**Library of Congress
Cataloging-in-Publication Data**
A World of luck / by the editors of Time-Life Books.
p.   cm.   (Library of curious and unusual facts).
Includes bibliographical references.
ISBN 0-8094-7711-4 (trade)
ISBN 0-8094-7712-2 (lsb)
1. Fortune—Anecdotes.
I. Time-Life Books. II. Series.
BF1778.W67 1991
133.3—dc20
91-7518 CIP

LIBRARY OF CURIOUS AND UNUSUAL FACTS

SERIES EDITOR: Laura Foreman
Series Administrator: Roxie France-Nuriddin
Art Director: Susan K. White
Picture Editor: Sally Collins

Editorial Staff for *A World of Luck*
Text Editors: John R. Sullivan (principal),
Sarah Brash
Associate Editor/Research: Vicki Warren
Assistant Editor/Research: Ruth Goldberg
Assistant Art Director: Alan Pitts
Senior Copy Coordinators: Jarelle S. Stein
(principal), Anthony K. Pordes
Picture Coordinator: Jennifer Iker
Editorial Assistant: Terry Ann Paredes

Special Contributors: William Barnhill, George
Constable, Don Oldenburg, Nancy Shute (text);
M. Tucker Jones Coombe, Edward O. Marshall,
Terrell D. Smith (research); Louise Wile (index)

Correspondents: Elisabeth Kraemer-Singh (Bonn),
Christine Hinze (London), Christina Lieberman (New
York), Maria Vincenza Aloisi (Paris), Ann Natanson
(Rome).
Valuable assistance was also provided by Angelika
Lemmer (Bonn); Judy Aspinall (London); Trini
Bandrés (Madrid); Elizabeth Brown, Katheryn White
(New York); Leonora Dodsworth, Ann Wise (Rome);
Dick Berry, Mieko Ikeda (Tokyo).

The Consultants:
William R. Corliss, the general consultant for the
series, is a physicist-turned-writer who has spent the
last twenty-five years compiling collections of
anomalies in the fields of geophysics, geology, ar-
chaeology, astronomy, biology, and psychology. He
has written about science and technology for NASA,
the National Science Foundation, and the Energy
Research and Development Administration (among
others). Mr. Corliss is also the author of more than
thirty books on scientific mysteries, including *Mysterious Universe, The Unfathomed Mind,* and *Hand-
book of Unusual Natural Phenomena.*

Ron Decker, curator of the Card Museum at the
United States Playing Card Company in Cincinnati,
Ohio, has done extensive research on the history of
playing cards.

Howard Schwartz is a gambling historian and the
marketing director of the Gamblers Book Club in
Las Vegas, Nevada, which offers a wide range of
books on gambling.

Marcello Truzzi, a professor of sociology at Eastern
Michigan University, is director of the Center for
Scientific Anomalies Research (CSAR) and editor of
its journal, *Zetetic Scholar.*

Alan Vaughn is a researcher and writer in the area
of parapsychology. For twenty years, Mr. Vaughn has
researched coincidences—many of which have been
published in his book *Incredible Coincidence.* Since
1980, he has been a consultant for the Los Angeles
based Mobius Society in applied ESP projects.

Other Publications:

THE NEW FACE OF WAR
HOW THINGS WORK
WINGS OF WAR
CREATIVE EVERYDAY COOKING
COLLECTOR'S LIBRARY OF THE UNKNOWN
CLASSICS OF WORLD WAR II
AMERICAN COUNTRY
VOYAGE THROUGH THE UNIVERSE
THE THIRD REICH
THE TIME-LIFE GARDENER'S GUIDE
MYSTERIES OF THE UNKNOWN
TIME FRAME
FIX IT YOURSELF
FITNESS, HEALTH & NUTRITION
SUCCESSFUL PARENTING
HEALTHY HOME COOKING
UNDERSTANDING COMPUTERS
LIBRARY OF NATIONS
THE ENCHANTED WORLD
THE KODAK LIBRARY OF CREATIVE PHOTOGRAPHY
GREAT MEALS IN MINUTES
THE CIVIL WAR
PLANET EARTH
COLLECTOR'S LIBRARY OF THE CIVIL WAR
THE EPIC OF FLIGHT
THE GOOD COOK
WORLD WAR II
HOME REPAIR AND IMPROVEMENT
THE OLD WEST

*For information on and a full description of any
the Time-Life Books series listed above, please ca
1-800-621-7026 or write:*
Reader Information
Time-Life Customer Service
P.O. Box C-32068
Richmond, Virginia 23261-2068

This volume is one in a series that explores
astounding but surprisingly true events in history,
science, nature, and human conduct. Other books
the series include:

Feats and Wisdom of the Ancients
Mysteries of the Human Body
Forces of Nature
Vanishings
Amazing Animals
Inventive Genius
Lost Treasure
The Mystifying Mind